"In looking in the mirror herself, Kathy turns it on us. We're not as strong and whole as the image we portray. In a gentle slap on the cheek, reminiscent of confirmation (pre-Vatican II), she interrupts our comfortability. The Divine Mystery is revealed. These stories and reflections invite us to accept our brokenness and be healed by the presence of God which awaits us behind a thousand disguises that Christ wears."

Leland D. Nagel
Executive Director for the National Conference of Catechetical Leadership (NCCL)
Washington, DC

"Kathy puts us right on the deck with her by letting us experience life in a L'Arche community. She shows us both the ways she has grown and the lessons she has learned from the core group at The Arch. She frankly reveals her own shortcomings and challenges while serving not simple folks who are continually grateful, but real people dealing with their own problems, concerns, and challenges. She draws from her experiences important spiritual lessons and insights about what it means to be a Christian. We can be grateful that Kathy chose to share her life with a L'Arche community and with us."

Anton Staley
Former editor of *The Compass*

"In *Walking on a Rolling Deck*, Kathleen Berken candidly shares her turbulent yet growth fulfilling ministry at the L'Arch Community in Clinton, Iowa. It is a personal journal that both reveals the journey of a soul as well as offers the reader a view of people who struggle with serious disabilities. Like the writings of Henri Nouwen, we have here honesty, realism, ambiguity, and a respect for the human condition."

Bishop Robert Morneau
Auxiliary Bishop of Green Bay
Pastor of Resurrection Parish

Walking on a Rolling Deck
Life on the Ark

Kathleen C. Berken

Foreword by
Jean Vanier

LITURGICAL PRESS
Collegeville, Minnesota

www.litpress.org

Names of all core members have been changed in order to protect their privacy.

Photographs: Copyright John Dylong 2008. Note: the photographs are all of L'Arche core members from across the United States, although not to be identified with the people within the stories. Guardians have given permission for the use of the core members' photographs.

Cover design by Ann Blattner.

Excerpt from *From Brokenness to Community* by Jean Vanier. Copyright © 1992, Paulist Press, Inc., New York/Mahwah, NJ. Reprinted by permission of Paulist Press, Inc. www.paulistpress.com

Scripture texts in this work are taken from the *New Revised Standard Version Bible* © 1989, Division of Christian Education of the National Council of the Churches of Christ in the United States of America. Used by permission. All rights reserved.

2	3	4	5	6	7	8

Library of Congress Cataloging-in-Publication Data

Berken, Kathleen C.
    Walking on a rolling deck : life on the ark / Kathleen C. Berken ;
foreword by Jean Vanier.
        p.   cm.
    Includes bibliographical references.
    ISBN 978-0-8146-1861-5
    1. Church work with people with mental disabilities—
Catholic Church—Anecdotes.   2. Church work with the developmentally
disabled—Catholic Church—Anecdotes.   3. Arche (Association)—
Anecdotes.   4. Group homes for people with mental disabilities—
Anecdotes.   5. Developmentally disabled—Anecdotes.   I. Title.

BX2347.8.M4B47   2008
267'.182—dc22   2008005838

To
Erica, Aaron, Sarah, and Isaac
and
The core members and assistants at
The Arch, L'Arche in Clinton, Iowa

Acknowledgments

Many persons are responsible for helping me fulfill my dream of publishing stories about the L'Arche community that gave me my life back. I am deeply grateful to these in particular:

- Jo Anne Horstmann, The Arch's community leader who hired me, and Eric Plaut, house coordinator at Arch I where I first lived, for their friendship and mentoring the deep spirituality of L'Arche

- Tony Staley, my editor and friend at *The Compass* at the Diocese of Green Bay where I worked for eleven years, who taught me how to write a decent sentence

- Lee Nagel, my dear friend who accompanies me on my L'Arche journey, for his compassion, understanding, wisdom, listening, love, and laughter

- The rest of my family, friends, and colleagues who shall here remain nameless, except in my heart, lest I leave out even one.

True stories from L'Arche, *a place where persons with and without intellectual and other developmental disabilities live in community and meet God face-to-face*

Contents

Foreword

Kathy, thank you for this book. Some people read books about L'Arche and pick up only those parts that seem beautiful, healing, and prayerful. They seem unable to see L'Arche as a place of pain that can lead us closer to Jesus.

You have lived and revealed in this book both sides, Kathy, and you show how what is painful can become beautiful. Those who have suffered rejection and contempt carry often within them a lot of hidden anger and violence that can at times explode. To be healed they need this anger to be accepted and held through forgiveness.

This book is about L'Arche as it really is—not a beautiful ideal but a reality that can be tiring and painful.

Jesus is truly living in the hearts of those who have been pushed aside. He is not just in gentle and prayerful liturgies but also in the mess of dailiness and of difficult relationships. The crucified Jesus leads to crucified people. The resurrection of Jesus leads us to discover the seeds of resurrection in all the pain of our world and in all the hidden pain in each of us. It leads us to celebration and to laughter. It is a place of healing for us all. Yes, you have well described life in a L'Arche home.

Jean Vanier
L'Arche
Trosly Breuil

The Beatitudes

When Jesus saw the crowds, he went up the mountain; and after he sat down, his disciples came to him. Then he began to speak, and taught them, saying:

"Blessed are the poor in spirit, for theirs is the kingdom of heaven.

"Blessed are those who mourn, for they will be comforted.

"Blessed are the meek, for they will inherit the earth.

"Blessed are those who hunger and thirst for righteousness, for they will be filled.

"Blessed are the merciful, for they will receive mercy.

"Blessed are the pure in heart, for they will see God.

"Blessed are the peacemakers, for they will be called children of God.

"Blessed are those who are persecuted for righteousness' sake, for theirs is the kingdom of heaven." (Matthew 5:1-10)

The Beatitudes are the opening of Jesus' Sermon on the Mount, which stretches from chapters 5 through 7 in

Matthew's gospel. These spiritual values are the foundation of L'Arche.

Henri Nouwen says: "The Beatitudes offer us a self-portrait of Jesus. At first it might seem to be a most unappealing portrait—who wants to be poor, mourning and persecuted? Who can be truly gentle, merciful, pure in heart, a peacemaker, and always concerned about justice? Where is the realism here? Don't we have to survive in this world and use the ways of the world to do so? Jesus shows us the way to be in the world without being of it. When we model our lives on his, a new world will open up for us."[1]

I grew up poor—and for a while, homeless—mourned the deaths of my parents shortly after college, and felt plenty of persecution as an angst-ridden, awkward teenager. I came to L'Arche as a single parent of two grown children with the pain of restlessness, believing that violence was more about the body and less about the spirit, and that revenge is just easier than forgiveness. My years in L'Arche have not been a panacea for those feelings. But living in L'Arche with men and women with disabilities has given me a deeper awareness of what it means to be blessed, and that wraps me in a warm coat to brave the biting winds and fierce storms I enter daily here. The awareness of blessedness—when it comes upon me, usually well after the storms have cleared—simply makes me smile. In that way there has been a change in my heart, and in my skin, my way of being in the world.

Introduction

L'Arche rhymes with "marsh" and means "ark" in French. Let's go with two meanings of ark for now: boat and covenant. I live at L'Arche in both senses of the word.

When God invited me to join him on this boat, I never imagined that I would encounter hurricane-force winds slamming against it, shoving it through such violent waves. "Really and truly?!" asks Mark. I live with him and four more men with cognitive disabilities whom we in L'Arche refer to as core members.

Yes, Mark, really and truly. I must have been facing the other way when the storm clouds began to gather. I never imagined getting beat up. Never imagined getting cancer. Never imagined being close to death. Never imagined finding God in persons we used to call "retarded." What a ride I was on. I don't know how Noah managed.

L'Arche was founded in 1964 by Jean Vanier in Trosly-Breuil, France, when this former philosophy professor and naval officer from Canada brought Raphael and Philipe from the horrors of their psychiatric institution to the safety of a home to live together as a Christian community.

Eight years later, the Benedictine Sisters of Erie, Pennsylvania, founded the first L'Arche community in the United States. The Arch, L'Arche in Clinton, Iowa, where I live, began in 1974 when Sister Marjorie Wisor, a Clinton Franciscan, invited Gerry Potter and Jim Kelleher—both now deceased—to live with her in a house borrowed from the local Presbyterian church. We're still borrowing that house.

"There is no doubt that The Arch was God's work," Sister Marjorie says. "It was one thing after another." The Arch was supposed to be in Davenport, and she was going to be only a start-up director, but the community ended up in Clinton, the same place as her motherhouse. She stayed for twelve years and fell in love with it. The best thing, she says, is the way L'Arche has grown throughout the world. "College groups and seminarians ask to come to live in the community, to immerse themselves in the upside-down value system the core members impart: primacy of relationships, relative unimportance of possessions, joy in living the present, readiness to forgive. It is wondrous to watch the abundant new life that God has created with such apparently insignificant ingredients."

As of this writing, there are 16 L'Arche communities in the United States and more than 130 in over 30 countries. Most are in France and Canada. Vanier said he never imagined L'Arche would grow so big. He likewise believes it is God's project, not his.

L'Arche is more than a series of group homes, or a federation of communities of faith, or a ministry to serve the poor, the neglected, the outcast. L'Arche is a gift from God wrapped in mystery. It's a place where we learn to be downright human. Some days it scares me to death. Other days I don't understand why I am so blessed. I've never felt deserving of this mystery.

The stories in this book are drawn from my daily life with the core members and the assistants who live and work with them. Vanier named them "core members" because *cor* is Latin for "heart," and they are the heart of L'Arche, the title of one of his books. The core members are L'Arche's gift, but I've learned never to be surprised at what I might discover when I remove the wrappings.

The gift of L'Arche is seeing God in core members' virtuous acts and even in their violent behaviors. I really do try to find God here. I pray every morning to see God's face, but sometimes God hides behind unimaginably poignant, sometimes absolutely absurd, and sometimes frighteningly horrific masks. I try to distinguish shadow from substance, illusion from truth.

I can identify with Mother Teresa who admitted in her journal[2] that she lived in utter darkness most of her life while serving God in Calcutta. The serpent of loneliness can and will slither up the tree of despair and hiss in your ear words of doubt that burrow deep into your soul. I've spent many a day sitting on my bed sobbing, feeling sorry for myself because I didn't believe anybody cared. Yet God was present. When

Gene, a core member, walks through the door after returning from his job at Skyline, a sheltered workshop (the term for an organization that provides supportive employment for persons with disabilities), and puts his arm around my shoulder and says, "I missed you when you were gone," the snake of self-pity returns to its lair. At least momentarily.

My hopes and dreams are no different from most: I want a life of peace and joy. That's the mission of L'Arche, Vanier says. "We can find the road to hope and peace in our world if we open ourselves to change, enter into true relationships, and break down the walls around our own hearts. I believe that even today, we can unleash a torrent of loving kindness that will bring peace to our world."[3]

Some days, though, the path to hope and peace is littered with potholes and broken glass. I believe that we live as family despite roadblocks of anger, violence, and pain. Caring for our core members' needs while helping them be independent is staggering. We do most everything: cook; shop; bathe; brush teeth; wipe butts; handle expenses; drive them to medical appointments; spend weekends at Special Olympics; write letters; do paperwork; communicate with family, guardians, and case managers; accompany them to church; plan outings; go to dances, the park, restaurants. But more, we hope to be friends. Yet hope can slam you in the face when, without warning, an angry core member threatens to kill you. That makes it challenging to be friends.

However, there are days when God does unleash torrents of loving kindness. After supper, we gather around our prayer table, light candles, dim lamps, play soft music, and sit back to ponder the day and maybe even sleep. God won't abandon us for resting in his heart. We pass the candle and each person has a chance to pray. Then we stand, hold hands, and recite the Lord's Prayer to bring closure to the day and unity to our house. Our prayers often include family and friends, apologies or requests. I usually pray for L'Arche communities, my friends, and family. I honestly don't know why I can't pray the way Don, a core member, does: "God, I want to hear a train go by. Amen."

Some stories in this book touch on sacred moments like that. Others may be tougher to read. I wrote about what's real in L'Arche. Living in a L'Arche community isn't always like taking a vacation with your lover God to an idyllic Caribbean beach. Some days it's more like climbing to the top of Mount Everest with God as your Sherpa, with times of feeling that the Sherpa has wandered off. But for those who have reached the top, well, I would imagine that they felt like Peter, James, and John when they witnessed the transfiguration of Jesus (Matt 17:1-8).

I haven't even reached base camp yet. I came to The Arch in 1999 as a single parent with two grown children, Aaron and Erica, six years after my divorce. Wow, I was in L'Arche, called by God to this new ministry of service, guided by the wisdom of Jean Vanier and Henri Nouwen, the latter who lived for ten years at the Daybreak L'Arche community in Toronto and often wrote of his experiences. It was so cool. I left almost everything behind, free to start a new life. I was going to live entirely for God with all these people who obviously needed me. I never thought I would ever again taste the bitterness of loneliness or despair. Was I ever wrong.

I learned that no matter where you go, you take your life with you. You can leave your stuff back there, but you can never leave your self behind. Unmet needs can be buried for a while, but they will start to decompose, rot, invite maggots. Left untreated, psychic time capsules can explode.

In deep denial of my buried needs, I dove headfirst into L'Arche. I learned routines and adjusted to the rhythm of the days—the endless work that desperately needed to be done, and my precious forty-five hours away each week.

Core members depended on me. Gertie called me "Mom"; Bill called me "Pal." I shopped, cooked, cleaned, and did laundry. I drove the van and counted money. I took the core members to church and on outings. But as my L'Arche family began to take root, I grew more lonely for my first family. Aaron and Erica visited for a few days. Their leaving ripped a hole in my heart. They returned at Easter and I hid eggs and baskets, just as when they were little. When they left, the hole in my heart grew larger.

Although L'Arche filled many of my needs for friends, support, community, security, love, affirmation, and a family, I continued to struggle with the heaviest burden: intimacy. Even writing about it scares me. As was probably true of most teens in the '60s, Simon and Garfunkel's "I

Am a Rock" was my theme song. Maybe it still is. "I have my walls and my poetry to protect me. . . ." I let only a few trusted people into my walled garden. Perhaps it's why being with core members is easy— they don't put demands on their love. Attachments with them are usually not so deep nor so messy as with other people. But they are real attachments.

On my worst days, my soul longs for spiritual connections and the loneliness feels like a boulder I am carrying all the way to the top of Mount Everest. I can be honest and open; I will tell the truth I see; I'm unpretentious with core members; and that all does spark some intimacy. But it's not enough. And why not? Because there are limits to intimacy with core members. For one thing, it's unethical and illegal (it would be considered adult dependent abuse) to form anything but friendships with them, and for another, I simply need a peer to be one with. But perhaps the gift of this emptiness is that it stretches my soul and pulls my heart apart to make room for God's grace.

We come to L'Arche with cracks and wounds. We come to L'Arche for an hour or a lifetime, for a reason that perhaps may be buried with us at death. Do we arrive on the ark to serve? Definitely. I think we also come to grow and to be healed. We'll all climb a mountain or two here.

I've discovered that if I have God as my Sherpa, my guide, I will live.

1
Ten Days and Counting

November 2, 1999

I've been here for ten days. That's it. Ten whole days. The community I was so excited about last summer is not the community I'm living in tonight. I'm lonely and sad. Bear with me. Please.

First, a few definitions: our community is called The Arch. We are a L'Arche (which means "the ark" in French) community which was founded by Jean Vanier in 1964 where people with cognitive disabilities (known as "core members") live with people who do not have such disabilities (known as "assistants"). The Arch is comprised of three houses (known as "Arch I," "Arch II," and "Arch III") and several apartments (known simply as our "apartment community") which are home to nineteen core members and a dozen or so full- and part-time assistants, six of whom live in the houses. All but two of our core members work at the local sheltered workshop in Clinton: Skyline Center, Inc.

19

Skyline Center works with local businesses to provide labor to do simple tasks for its clients, such as attaching bar-code stickers to plastic connectors or machine parts, clipping bags of pet-food samples to displays for veterinarian offices, or breaking down and bundling boxes for recycling. The companies do not want to pay full wages or purchase expensive machines for these jobs. Clients at Skyline Center receive training and support in addition to lower wages. Some sheltered workshops also receive federal monies through the Medicaid Waiver program for assisting persons with disabilities.

I went out to Skyline Center this morning for a tour and a visit and got a giant group hug from the core members I know. That place is something else. When I walked in and saw the core members from The Arch, I felt like a rock star. They all came over and stood around me, reaching out their arms and hugging me all at once. Yeah, it was great.

But here is the self-pitying news: this afternoon, I had almost no time to rest before heading over to Arch III for dinner, evening activities, prayer, and bedtime routines. I was very tired as I walked into an environment at that house that needed all my energy and attention. There was dinner to fix, letter-writing with the core members, brushing their teeth, and helping them with other bedtime routines. I did not have enough for them and me. As a result of not being able to give 100 percent, and a host of other reasons, I am right now feeling lonely and sad even after all those hugs and that celebrity greeting this morning.

I struggle with having to also create wide open spaces for the assistants, who sometimes seem to be more needy than some of the core members. Apparently, this is what God is giving me this week, but, trust me, this wasn't in the L'Arche brochure when I signed up. Not this.

When I came here I had this fantastically idealistic notion that God sent me to live for a while on this ark, and I had an image in my head of people like me walking up the gangplank, meeting God at the top, and being given a clipboard with the day's assignment on it. I saw myself roaming around the ark, bumping into all kinds of people, going into room after room, encountering some people who were having fun and others crying, staying with them for a while, checking off my hourly assignments. Then God would gather all the assistants together at night and we would discuss our day and then we would go over our L'Arche assignments. I saw myself going to sleep peacefully and joyfully, knowing that I lived well through my day's lessons and I'd be getting a new list tomorrow from The Captain.

That's a wonderful fantasy—to be the cruise director with a loveboat smile pasted on my face—but I can't live it because the ark I'm on is rolling and heaving and I'm sick to my stomach, not to mention sad and lonely. I feel like the galley slave, the grunt who swabs the deck, the second to last to go down with the ship.

Everything I thought about L'Arche is bogus. Am I really here to understand, to listen, to accept everyone's brokenness, even the assistants who are here to serve the core members? I don't want this. I want the fantasy of being on the ark with God—clipboard in hand, schmoozing with the passengers—and not feeling all this pain. I came here to serve the core members, the people with disabilities, the ones Jean Vanier says are broken and weak, the ones God gave us to find the Divine Mystery through the cracks in their spirits. I came here to serve the people with disabilities who have been rejected and scorned and hated just for being different. I did not come here to serve the assistants! We're supposed to be the strong ones.

I'm feeling disillusioned and the feeling isn't good. I am also feeling way too sorry for myself. I miss my friends in Green Bay, and it's taking too long to make new friends. I know ten days isn't long. It takes time to start over, I try to tell myself, but tonight I am having one hell of a time processing that.

I heard a story once about a woman who found her inner strength by painting a brilliant sunset and then giving it away to a stranger unsigned. But the more I think about it and the image it portends, it's just too preachy. Oh, paint a sunset. Remove yourself from the picture. Give it away so your ego doesn't get out of control. Too preachy. I hate preachy.

Ten days into my new life, I am starting to question why God called me to this L'Arche community. I'm tired. Work here never ends. I'm not that strong. But if God is trying to empty me of myself and asking me—no, *making* me—listen to broken, unintelligible speech and tend to weak hearts and understand limited abilities, and teach me patience while I'm doing it, then, God, you're doing a fantastic job. Way to go, God.

Really, I don't do much. For now, I wash core members' hair in the kitchen sink, help people make and send cards to their friends and families, cook dinner, clean up, brush core members' teeth, help with laundry, clean toilets, mop floors, go shopping, fix torn clothing, settle differences. I am nearing the end of my two-week orientation at Arch III. Although my room is at Arch I, where I've been assigned, I still have two weeks of orientation at Arch II before I can officially start my life at Arch I.

As I write this, it's late. I need to sleep. I have finished my day's work at Arch III. I am back in my room at Arch I, constantly being interrupted by Gertie, a core member who has been in and out of my room ten times, hugging me goodnight, which I think is part of her never-ending bedtime routine. She talks constantly, but usually it's not to anybody in particular. She talks to herself, to her clothes, her headbands, to anything she sees in front of her. She has no unspoken thought or feeling, and she is very hard of hearing, but she won't wear her hearing aids at home, so I have to shout into her ear for her to hear. Then she says, "Don't shout at me!" when I try to repeat what I said because she says she can't hear me.

Gertie's need for hugs and attention has begun to irritate me because she is interrupting my writing and I think she needs to go to bed. She will spend the next hour setting the table for tomorrow's breakfast, brushing her gums, assembling her clothes and jewelry—those dime-store white plastic beads she wears everywhere— putting away her stuff, talking to the things in her drawers and closet, and coming in here, saying goodnight a hundred more times.

I battle the brokenness here. It's my personal war on the woundedness in every person—core member and assistant. We encounter each other's vulnerabilities every day, and as a new assistant I'm a safe stranger to assistants who find it easy to open up to a person they don't have any history with. Maybe they have told their stories dozens of times to anybody who will listen, or maybe they have not been able to talk to anybody else about their frustrations with the community.

Now, along with feeling sad and lonely, I feel arrogant and egotistical. I have to admit, I'm not that good. So tonight, at least for this night, I will just give it all to God, because, really, I need to sleep. And I have yet to resolve any of my feelings.

My tenth day on the ark and all the good I have to show for it is some attention at Skyline, interacting and helping core members at Arch III, and a constant flow of hugs and goodnight's from that little woman Gertie who lives with me.

Somebody please tell me, where the hell was the Divine Mystery today?

I hear sounds up on the deck. I suppose I should go see what they want. Heck, I can sleep later.

But Noah found favor in the sight of the LORD. . . . I will establish my covenant with you; and you shall come into the ark, you, your sons, your wife, and your sons' wives with you. (Genesis 6:8, 18)

2 Christmas Morning with Gertie

December 25, 1999

When I woke up on Christmas morning, 1999, a couple months after I arrived at The Arch, all I thought about were all the Christmases I spent with my own parents and brothers, as well as the years I was with my own family and children. I lay in bed, eyes wide open, and grew terribly nostalgic for the cozy Christmas mornings of my past where we would open presents and then sit down to a very special breakfast of scrambled eggs, pork sausage, and homemade Christmas coffee cake. But here at The Arch Christmas breakfasts were nothing more than the usual fare of cereal or leftovers. I knew that we would be having a big turkey dinner later at another house, and so I tried to talk myself into believing that I didn't need my old traditions. I was in L'Arche now. We have new traditions. I lectured myself: "Forget your special breakfasts of Christmas pasts; you're serving the core members now."

27

I was not happy. I was miserable. I felt terribly sorry for myself. I got out of bed and headed to the basement to take my shower. I spotted a pot of bean soup on the stove and was resigned to the fact that last night's dinner would be my special breakfast. So much for coffee cake, sausage, and eggs. Some Christmas this is turning out to be. Ugh. What a Scrooge I was, but so what? Christmas has its traditions and I was fifty years old and for the first time in my life would not celebrate Christmas as I always did. Pity parties usually don't need invitations.

After my shower, I walked back through the kitchen and core member Gertie stopped me and pointed to the kitchen table. "Kathy, I want to show you something," she said. I looked over at the table, and noticed that she had set a place for me with my favorite plate and a small bowl, a container of cottage cheese, two pieces of toast, my favorite mug filled with water, a little jelly glass with orange juice, the butter container, and a knife and spoon. She called over to me and said, "I made you breakfast."

She pointed to the table with both hands as if to make a presentation, smiled, and said again, "I did this all for you." I walked over, sat down, and just looked at everything. She sat across from me and watched, still smiling. I scooped out some cottage cheese, mixed it with a little applesauce, and spread butter on the toast, which by now was cold and hard, but she didn't know that and I didn't care. I looked across the table at her and she said, "I am serving you now."

I looked out the window at the snow on the evergreen bushes and the trees. The sun was shining and it was Christmas morning, and when I looked down at my plate, I could hardly see my food. As I finished various parts of my meal, Gertie would get up and stand by me and ask, "Are you done?" I'd say "Yes, I am," and so, dish by dish, she cleared the table. I drank my juice, ate my toast, and finished the cottage cheese. It didn't matter if I might not be hungry for turkey and all the trimmings two hours later. A woman with no teeth and a huge heart and more hugs to offer than any person clinically needs in a day graced me with the best Christmas present in the world.

I saw God today and God fed me. If this isn't Eucharist, I don't know what is.

Jesus said to them, "I am the bread of life. Whoever comes to me will never be hungry, and whoever believes in me will never be thirsty." (John 6:35)

3 Why Am I Here?

January 11, 2000

The core members are bugging me. All of them. I've been here for ten weeks. The fantasy that living in L'Arche would be as easy and fun as the one-week visit I made last summer evaporated as fast as breath on a mirror at high noon in a desert. I should not have been surprised. Maybe I'm just homesick. My friends from Green Bay have been telling me how much they miss me. Some want me to come home. Why am I here, anyway? Why did I leave my good job writing for *The Compass*, the Catholic diocesan newspaper, and all my friends to come to this little Mississippi River town to live in a house with people who have disabilities? To find a family again after the divorce, after my own children grew up and moved away? Couldn't I have found a group home to work in up there?

Obviously not. Because, obviously, that's not what God had in mind. Dear God.

Let me tell you what's going on with the core members here at Arch I. Right now we have only three because Elaine moved into a supervised apartment last August, a couple months before I arrived. We are looking for a fourth core member. Currently I live with core members Bill, Gertie, and Sam. The house coordinator, Eric, also lives here.

Bill has a crude side to him, to put it kindly, which he inherited from the string of institutions where he lived for forty-seven years before settling into The Arch eight years ago. At age fifty-six, he is here on the ark with me. God help me.

Is my relationship with him going to be menacing, magical, or mysterious? What do I expect from him? I am scared of this man who uses clear, obscene gestures and a mean tone of voice suggesting violence. He practically barks at people when he wants to hurt them, when he's crabby, wants a cigarette, or feels threatened, even by the presence of a new person in the house. I understand it and yet I am offended by his trash talk and afraid of his penchant for violent outbursts. I don't ever want to get used to this. I doubt that we will ever be friends. The best I am hoping for is that we can live civilly in this house. Good luck, pal.

I've discovered that the hardest work isn't the stuff we do day-to-day. We shop, clean, shovel snow, rake leaves, and do routine house maintenance, but the days and nights are long; and living with the core members in community, trying to build relationships with them, drains me emotionally. Is this what Jean Vanier meant when he said our weaknesses mirror each other's weaknesses? He said we would discover ourselves in the poor. We would uncover our sins, our fragmented souls, our broken hearts, and then we would point to the core members and ask God to change them, to fix their brokenness, to make them whole so we could live with them. But the true meaning of L'Arche is starting to become clear. Making people whole or fixing their cognitive disabilities is not what L'Arche is about. It's not why God created this community. The reasons go deeper than simply caring for people who can't care for themselves.

L'Arche is a place where we find ourselves. Many of us have somehow lost our way and are in search of a way home. We come to L'Arche with cracks in our very essence from years of rejection or feeling inadequate, with fresh wounds bleeding from our center after being abandoned and hurt by people we trusted, with almost-permanent marks on our beings from years of abuse, and feeling like we will fall apart if somebody touches us just one more time. We arrive in L'Arche and find scraps of ripped clothing on the floors of our souls, shards of broken glass stuck in our hearts, drops of dried paint spattered on the walls of our psyches, and bits of rusted metal crumbling from our spirits. We begin to interact with each other, and with focused attention, as we paint a spiritual picture of the core members, we identify with their issues and we focus on their weaknesses because they are our own. Then, oh yes, that's when the trouble begins.

People with cognitive disabilities often have involuntary behaviors, including constant chatter, tapping, or head and other body movements such as clapping or twitching. These things distract me at best and irritate me at worst. Their daily demands wear on me; their sins become mirrors that reflect my brokenness. But there is grace here, and I will take anything from God I can get. When I have accepted and understood L'Arche, I trust that I will see each core member as a projection of myself, and as much as I don't enjoy seeing myself as stubborn and crabby, this is how core members in L'Arche teach us.

We all breathe the same air. We all have atoms and molecules that were contained in each other's bodies. We are one, and more, we are all one in God. When that moment of awareness happens, it will be the moment in which the flood waters recede, the sun rises over the ark, the rainbow appears through the mist, and the dove with an olive branch in its beak flies overhead. It will be a moment of serendipity, when I will discover that God has been here all along.

That's the theory.

But here's how I actually live in L'Arche.

Meet Gertie. She's a four-foot ten-inch tall, fifty-five-year-old lovable woman with Down syndrome who has a great need for affection and has keen social skills to make friends easily and to speak readily about her life. Gertie is a diligent worker. She sets the table, folds and puts away towels, cleans the kitchen, reorganizes the dining room, dusts the furniture, makes salads, and helps cook. But she has her shadows. She is obsessive and fiercely stubborn. When she doesn't get her way, she digs in her heels. That bugs me. I don't know how to handle this behavior. I can't let her rule the house, but I also want to accept Gertie for being Gertie. I understand how being that short probably caused her to fight for her dignity and independence all her life, especially in the institution where she lived for thirty years before coming to The Arch eight years ago.

I am slowly discovering that the core members are my teachers. As a former math teacher, I learned some things from my students, but I never would have imagined that living with people with disabilities would be a classroom. So, interacting with Gertie causes me to recall times I needed a hug and, given my own need for affection, which I seldom show, one often isn't enough. I recall the times I was stubborn and how I would keep asking for what I wanted until I got it. I wonder how many people are irritated with my obsessions? More than I care to know.

In a couple of months, we will welcome Marilyn into our home. She is fifty years old and has lived as a recluse in her home her entire adult life. Her mother passed away only a few weeks ago and her sister and brothers sought a new home for Marilyn. We had an opening, and after meeting her, we quickly felt she could live well here. She will spend several weeks visiting us for longer periods of time, and then do an overnight, and then a few days in a row, to acclimate her to living here full time.

I saw a photo of Marilyn when she was eighteen. In the picture she is standing next to Jackie, a core member now at Arch II, who was about eight at the time. I was surprised that Jackie, who is forty, hasn't changed much. Marilyn was smiling in the picture, but now she is withdrawn, depressed, almost shrunken, and lives almost entirely inside herself. I wonder if she created this personality so she could cope with living as a shut-in all these years. I see stubbornness and shyness in Marilyn, but not much else. Certainly we believe there's a personality in there somewhere, one that caused her to smile in the photo, but at the moment we can't seem to reach her joyful spirit.

I think of the times when I was withdrawn, lonely, depressed; times when I lived inside myself and didn't want to come out. How many people did I confuse or hurt because of my neuroses? Did I even know?

Sam is the youngest core member in the house at age forty-eight. At six feet and two hundred thirty pounds, with a loud and persistent voice, he scares me. His vocal and emotional intensity, his almost constant angry demeanor and incessant talking and storytelling, make me feel like running away every time he's near me. He asks the same questions and says the same things, over and over, until I want to plug my ears and pretend he isn't there. I have tried to understand his speech, his attitude, his behaviors. I have tried to believe that his storytelling, his bragging, his incessant talking is simply his way of communicating— and it probably is— but he is wearing me out.

I think of the people who have interrupted me because I kept talking, the people who threw up their hands in frustration because I kept asking the same questions over and over, even when they couldn't give me any other answers. I think of the times I wouldn't be quiet either. Trouble is, I am still this way. Difficult as it is to admit, this is why I need to be Sam's student.

Perhaps, then, these are reasons God called me here to L'Arche, reasons written in fine print on the back of my L'Arche ticket, my qualifications to engage in this ministry of learning. Core members on the ark wear teacher's hats. They are no doubt completely oblivious to this, as they go about living their lives, holding invisible mirrors toward me. They will continue to hold those mirrors close to my face—mirrors I would rather see as clear glass—until the critical moment when I realize that the reason I can't see through the glass is because the back has a layer of silver. When I see myself in their eyes, when I realize that I am they, when I believe that God loves every single human being regardless, that's when I can be healed and when I will experience God's real presence.

A difficult truth in L'Arche is this: core members aren't here to change. Some may never be any different from the day I walked onto the gangplank of the ark and into this community. But perhaps, just perhaps, at some critical moment in my time here, I will see myself in them and I will make a conscious decision to change, and then perhaps

I will experience them with a different heart. That's the moment when they will change, too.

Jean Vanier speaks of L'Arche as a place of refuge and of hope, of trial and challenge. It's not poetry. It's real stuff.

I have a lot of work to do.

They came to Bethsaida. Some people brought a blind man to him and begged him to touch him. He took the blind man by the hand and led him out of the village; and when he had put saliva on his eyes and laid his hands on him, he asked him, "Can you see anything?" And the man looked up and said, "I can see people, but they look like trees, walking." Then Jesus laid his hands on his eyes again; and he looked intently and his sight was restored, and he saw everything clearly. (Mark 8:22-25)

4 Footwashing

January 21, 2000

Lent will soon be upon us, and I think of the footwashing on Holy Thursday. And even though L'Arche communities everywhere simply and powerfully ritualize that washing of the feet, I have discovered that even if I never take soap and rag to anyone's foot, I am supposed to be washing their feet.

When I zip up Dayton's coat or wash Vincent's soiled underwear or Sam's wet sheets, when I brush Mark's teeth for him at night or help Bill shave in the morning, I am supposed to be washing their feet.

Henri Nouwen spoke often of sacred moments in L'Arche at the Daybreak community near Toronto where he lived and worked as an assistant and as the pastor of the community for ten years until his death in 1996. He spoke once of helping a core member each night hang up his belt on a hook, that this was a holy moment.

Hearing that was a holy moment for me, too. I was taken.

But I am arrogant and life here offers me many doses of humility. I do nothing here that many others have not done as parents, caregivers, and friends. Many have done way more than I will ever do here in L'Arche. They care for sick and dying and disabled people, they live more like Blessed Mother Teresa of Calcutta who picked up dying people on the street one at a time because, she said, that's how she found Jesus. They live with spouses and parents with Alzheimer's Disease for twenty-four hours a day seven days a week without respite.

So, I dare not speak of my little mundane tasks as holy if I cannot see what others do as even more holy. I am merely tying shoes. I am merely zipping up coats. I am merely brushing teeth. I am shaving faces and combing hair. Others sit day after day after day with dying AIDS patients. They live and work in homeless shelters with people who have mental illnesses and are not on state-funded medications, have no health insurance. They go into war-devastated countries and hold and care for men and women whose bodies are blown half-apart by bombs and bullets that by somebody's twisted imaginations were manufactured to bring peace on earth.

I have discovered this much: nobody washes anybody's feet as Jesus did unless there is dirt stuck way under their fingernails and embedded in the deep cracks in their skin. You can't wash off the dirt, and sometimes you don't even try. Instead, the brave ones go back and tend to bleeding bodies, scoop up constant gushes of vomit, scrape sick and dying people's shit from their beds, and can only hold their hands and embrace their very broken bodies until death mercifully takes them home.

That, I believe, is washing feet as Jesus did. I do none of this, and I ache for those who find rivers of mud beneath them as they wash the feet of the people God sends. These are the people who have my heart. All of it.

And so I cry for the people with filthy feet who beg us to make them clean, and then I look at our core members, whose feet I barely wash by the tiny gestures of care I give them. And that's when the truth hits me, like a rock tied in an old rag that crashes through my window and shatters the glass into a million shards.

Listen to my truth. Listen carefully. I am not here in this L'Arche community to wash anybody's feet. That is not why God invited me here. God called me here so someone could make me sit down on a hard-backed chair and ask me to take off my shoes and my socks and bare my ugly stinky feet to this whole L'Arche community, so that all the scars, bruises, and smells of my life might be brought out into the open. It is the core members who then walk up to me, and in all the weakness and brokenness and all the disabilities Jean Vanier has pointed out to me again and again, kneel down, scoop up a handful of water, let it spill through their clumsy hands over my feet and onto the floor. That's when I shut my eyes and cover my face because I cannot bear to watch them do this. I cry because I thought in my arrogance that I came here to serve, but no, they are serving me, and my pride can't bear the weight.

When Betsy walks up behind me quietly and gently wraps her arms around me and leans her head into my back and says, "My puppy, Kathy," I turn around to see her smile and I am humbled by the footwashing of affection.

When I walk through Skyline and all the core members from The Arch and dozens of other folks shout out "Hi, Kathy!" as I pass their work stations, I am humbled by the footwashing of welcome.

When I fell onto the concrete floor in the basement of Arch I after hitting my head again on that vent pipe overhead, and Sam asked, "Are you all right?" and reached his hand down and I took it and he lifted me up, and then later at dinner he asked again, "Are you okay?" I am humbled by the footwashing of compassion.

The core members in my community have far more dirt under their fingernails and far more mud in the cracks of their skin than I ever would have imagined.

After he had washed their feet, had put on his robe, and had returned to the table, he said to them, "Do you know what I have done to you? You call me

Teacher and Lord—and you are right, for that is what I am. So if I, your Lord and Teacher, have washed your feet, you also ought to wash one another's feet. For I have set you an example, that you also should do as I have done to you." (John 13:12-15)

5 Bill in the Afternoon
January 26, 2000

I never thought that I would like Bill. He is a core member whose life is peppered with violence, meanness, and coarseness. But sometimes moments of grace collide head-on with moments of pain. Sometimes somebody with a knot in his shoes looks up at me and makes a noise that sounds like "help me," and at that very moment, hard as it is to believe, I can see better, my hands are warmer, my heart pumps faster. There I am, looking into God's face, unknotting a shoelace. I cannot understand it, but in the deepest part of my soul, I know the truth: this is the God of my birth, the God of my heart, the God of my longing.

Supernatural experiences of this sort don't happen very often, trust me. What happened tonight is an experience that brought back my heart.

When Bill came home from work today, I asked him how his day was and he said, "Fine." I looked at his notebook from work where a supervisor wrote "Good day," and I took a deep breath and smiled at him. "Great job, Bill!" Bill, however, went right to his task. He didn't even take off his coat, because as soon as he was done with his chores he would get a cigarette and go outside to smoke. There's no point in wasting time taking off a coat if you're just going to put it back on in a few minutes because, for Bill, cigarettes don't want to wait for a coat.

Bill was focusing on putting away the dishes. It hadn't taken long for me to discover that cigarettes are great motivators. Bill carefully picked up a plate from the drain rack, walked three feet, opened a cupboard door, and set the plate carefully on the stack. Then he walked back to the rack and took another plate, repeated the same steps, and carefully set that one on top of the last. On and on, one dish at a time. It never occurred to Bill to pick up a few plates and stack them together first so he could get finished faster. This behavior is one of the signs of mental retardation I find curious. When there is a job to be done of any sort, from putting away dishes to taking a bath, most of our folks work at the task in individual segments, and speed is generally not important, unless you're Mark, a core member who does everything from eating to cleaning to making his bed with lightning speed. Both of these men teach me the value of patience.

For Bill, finding homes for all the dishes on the rack has been a challenge because some dishes aren't as easily identified as "plate," "cereal bowl," "drinking glass," or "coffee cup." What would you do with a mortar and pestle? If you were Bill, you wouldn't put them together. You'd put the mortar with the bowls and the pestle with the wooden spoons. Makes sense to me, too.

After Bill finished putting away the dishes, he found me and said, "Done," which means he wants a cigarette and it's my turn to do something. He put two fingers up to his lips as the sign for cigarette, and he was in such a good mood after having a good day at work, I felt like teasing him a little first. I'm starting to understand Bill's brand of humor. He laughs readily at slapstick. Frankly, I don't see the humor in people falling down or getting a pie thrown in their face, but I want to connect with Bill, so I tried something different.

I put my left hand squarely on his shoulder and my right index finger on his chest, as if to poke him, and looking him straight in the eye with a tough, low, James Cagney–like thug voice, I said, "Okay, Bill, what did you do with all those dishes? Huh? Did you throw them in the snowbank? Huh? Huh!? C'mon, Bill, fess up or I'll have to toss you in the brig and throw away the key."

Startled, he just looked at me. He didn't seem sure if I was serious or kidding, but I held my gaze and then he started to smile, and then he laughed. So loud I thought he was going to pop his dentures right out of his mouth. I took my hand from his shoulder and stood back a little and turned toward the file cabinet. I opened the drawer and let him choose a miniature plastic football helmet.

We get these from a vending machine and when Bill has a good day at work, this is his reward. He took the helmet and then immediately handed it back so I could snap the little face mask onto the sides. He stood waiting patiently, and when I was finished, instead of handing it to him, I plopped it on the top of my head and looked at him seriously. He looked at that little plastic toy on top of my head and laughed again.

I was on a roll. I opened the drawer where we keep his cigarettes and I took one out and pretended that it was my cigarette and I was starting to put it in my mouth and casually said, "Bill, it's cold outside. I'll just smoke this for you so you don't have to go out in the cold." He laughed again, but was tiring of the jokes and wanted his cigarette. He took it out of my hand, turned around, and went outside for his smoke.

Why did it take me so long to figure out how easy it is to make Bill happy?

Five minutes later Bill walked back into the house, took off his coat, and, completing the afternoon ritual, said he wanted a cup of coffee. I continued to tease him and in a complaining voice whined, "Bill, you want everything, don't you? First you come in the house and you don't take off your coat, and then you hide the dishes outside in the snow, and then you want a helmet, and then a cigarette, and *now* what do you want? A cup of coffee?!" He laughed again, and he reached for his favorite Green Bay Packer coffee cup, filled it with water, and took it to the microwave.

Together we pushed the buttons and he came back and got out the jar of instant coffee and a spoon.

While we waited for the water to get hot, I felt something stir in me that Jean Vanier said would come to us if we were tuned into L'Arche on a deep level. I looked at Bill and suddenly felt a deep connection with him, even though when we met he was angry, distant, and downright mean to me. The first few months at The Arch I went to my room most nights and cried because I wanted to live in peace with these people and Bill's mistrust of me hurt my heart every day. But this afternoon, in this moment, in this time and in this place, I saw God's face in Bill's.

God invited me to L'Arche and Bill invited me to live it. With his anger, his mistrust, and his daily rejection, Bill instructed me to keep going anyway. He instructed me to trust and to love regardless. He taught me the value of slapstick.

I learned to love Bill, but even more, I learned to like him. Love is a task that takes time, effort, and commitment. Sometimes love just isn't something I feel, it's something I do. But to like somebody, that carries a different commitment and can lead to friendship. I knew something amazing was about to happen when Bill and I laughed together. You just can't be friends with someone if you have never laughed at the same thing together.

Someday when we are both in heaven and are looking for something to do, perhaps I will sit down with Bill over a cup of coffee and he will explain to me what it felt like to have inhabited that body all those years. His stories may surprise me. He might have known more about what it means to be human than I ever dreamed possible.

Deal bountifully with your servant,
*   so that I may live and observe your word.*
Open my eyes, so that I may behold
*   wondrous things out of your law.* (Psalm 119:17-18)

6 What Happened to Bill's Toe?

January 26, 2000

I can hardly believe the pain Bill can suffer without complaining. After prayer time in the living room tonight we stood in a circle, as is our custom, held hands, and prayed the Lord's Prayer. Bill could hardly stand up.

"Does your back hurt?" I asked him.

"No," he said.

His face tightened and he grimaced in pain. I asked him again, "Are you okay?"

"No, my foot," he responded in an anguished voice.

"Please sit down and take off your slippers," I said. Just under his big toe was a wide cut. Ouch. He reached down and pulled back his toe a little so I could see. The cut was so deep it went through all the layers of skin. I thought I was going to faint.

This is not good. The foot nor the fainting. I'd be a great nurse. Yeah. Mention the word "blood" and I could be on the floor in ten seconds. Maybe less. According to an internet article I found, this condition affects about 4 percent of the population.

Any talk of blood, much less the sight of it, sends me into a spin. My hands get clammy, my heart beats faster, my vision blurs, I get light-headed, and if I don't put my head between my knees or lie down so my feet are higher than my heart, I'm gone. Out in sixty seconds. I'm not proud of this, especially when I have to help somebody who is injured, even if it's only to bandage a toe.

Medical personnel love people like me. I once was called to the hospital when my son Aaron was taken there after hitting his head on the floor while playing basketball. I walked in and saw him lying on a gurney with a bright orange foam brace on his head. I started to imagine the worst and I passed out. Now they had to deal with two patients, so they made me register and check in with a doctor. You should have seen me when I was a camp counselor on the day the girls learned how to sharpen their scout knives. I'm not kidding, I don't want to talk about it.

My face was six inches from Bill's toe, which looked as if a knife had sliced the bottom half and it was ready to come off. I gasped and sat hard on the floor so I'd be closer in case my body was going to keep going. "My God, Bill, what happened to you?!" Gertie and Sam were hovering over us, repeatedly asking, "What's wrong with Bill? What's wrong with Bill?" I quickly decided to deal with this before I became a medical disaster. So, I said, "Bill cut his toe and I'm going to fix it." As any good medical professional would do, I asked Sam to go into the kitchen and get a glass of water. It gave me a chance to breathe. Gertie didn't move. She stood watch over Bill to be sure he was okay. She was protecting me, too, although she didn't know it.

I asked Bill if he could walk into the kitchen. He said, "Yeah," so I followed him as he limped into the kitchen, and I pulled out a chair for him to sit on. As any good medical professional would do, I filled the dishpan with hot water and set it on the floor in front of Bill and asked him to put his foot in it. I sat on the floor in front of him, just in case.

"How does that feel?" I asked, and he said, "Fine." Next I decided to clean the wound, which wasn't bleeding, thank God. I found a bottle of baby shampoo with a Winnie-the-Pooh head for a cap and dumped the little that was left into the water. Bill asked if he could have the cap. How ironic that a man with a history of anger and violence wanted a plastic Winnie-the-Pooh.

And then, instead of passing out from the sight of that dangling toe, I suddenly became aware of something amazing. When Bill asked me for the Winnie-the-Pooh head, I immediately saw a side of Bill that was completely hidden before. I saw his innocence, the little boy in him that let me tend to his sore foot and asked if he could have a child's toy.

I stayed sitting on the floor in front of him and washed his foot, teasing him with a couple of visual images that lightened the moment for Bill and the others, and further helped keep me from thinking too much about his toe and becoming, yes, a medical specimen myself. I said in a serious, low, doctorlike tone, "Bill, I think I will have to do some surgery here. I will have to cut off your leg. You don't need your leg, do you? You have two of them. Isn't that correct, sir?"

He held his hand over his mouth to keep his dentures from falling out while he was laughing so hard at the image I just painted. Gertie walked into the kitchen and asked me, "Is he going to live?" and I immediately went serious again. "No, probably not. We can have the funeral tomorrow." I turned to Bill and said, "That would be okay, wouldn't it Bill? You're not doing anything special tomorrow, are you? We can bury you in the morning, right after breakfast. And since you won't be here, I'll just eat your cereal, okay?" He laughed even louder.

Bill is so easy to entertain.

I lifted his foot out of the water and tried to dry it off with the towel, but even though he didn't seem to feel the cut on his toe, the rest of his foot was sensitive to the touch. So he kept pulling it away as I rubbed the towel over it. He'd drop his foot into the water and it would splash so I teased him. "Bill, you're getting me all wet! Okay, I'm just going to have to arrest you. Where are those handcuffs?" He was laughing again.

Determined to get this finished, I sat cross-legged on the floor in front of him and rested his foot on my knee.

I was having fun, and so was he. I told him that I could tickle him without even touching him. "Watch this," I said. He was ready and held his hand over his mouth again to protect me from flying dentures. I put my finger about an inch from his foot and, without touching him at all, I drew an imaginary line in the air down the length of his foot. He howled. I was serious: "Bill, as your doctor, I have a diagnosis for this foot. It needs to come off tonight. I'm sorry, but we will have to operate." His laugh was so loud he could have scared the neighborhood.

Tending to feet and learning how to make people laugh when they are in pain are just two of the things I am learning here. My constant search for deeper connections is elusive. Tonight's God-incidence was serendipitous, a few minutes stolen from space and time, completely unsought. At least consciously. These are the sacred moments of L'Arche.

I walked with Bill to his room as he limped up the stairs and I told him, in all sincerity, "Bill, your toe will feel much better in the morning." But then I teased, "Do you want me to kiss it?" He laughed. "No, Bill, I'm sorry, as your doctor, I can't kiss your toe." We found his pajamas and I helped him change: this fifty-six-year-old gruff of a man who, at least for now, was a kindly old grandpa. I slipped a clean white sock onto his injured foot and told him that in the morning, after his shower, he was not to put socks or shoes on, but to let me change the bandage first. I said, "Okay?" He said, "Okay." I checked to be sure he was settled in,

walked to the door, turned and smiled. "Good night, Bill,"
I whispered. He smiled back. "Night," he said.

*Mary took a pound of costly perfume made of pure
nard, anointed Jesus' feet, and wiped them with her
hair. The house was filled with the fragrance of the
perfume.* (John 12:3)

7 World Youth Day in Rome
August 2000

Ten months after my arrival at The Arch, I went to Rome with my children, Aaron and Erica, for World Youth Day, a trip we had planned for two years. The two weeks were magical and I was thrilled to spend this time with my children and a million and a half other young adults. It was a good break from life in L'Arche, a time to reconnect with my children and some old friends from Green Bay.

While there, I tried to stay present to each experience to remember every sound, smell, taste, and sight from St. Peter's Basilica to the Coliseum to the bistros. I had been in the Eternal City twenty years before when I was married, but this trip was very different. I went as an adult chaperone on a pilgrimage meant for young adults who were, for the most part, coming of age in their religious and spiritual imaginations. Most had never traveled outside their own countries and almost none of them had ever seen the pope.

Pope John Paul II was their hero and they responded to him as they would their favorite rock star, with whoops, whistles, and clamors of love from afar.

For me, the time in Rome affirmed my role as mom. Erica and I grew closer as we laughed at the mysteries of a Roman hotel room complete with a shower that sprayed water over the entire bathroom. Her let's-have-as-much-fun-as-possible personality pushed away my tendency toward seriousness and tagged me as the group's mom. One afternoon on a bus ride to Florence, I found myself in the middle of a detailed discussion with several other young adults on the many uses of the bidet. And to the young man who wanted more information on how males were to use it, I simply said, "Trial and error solves a great many mysteries in life." They all laughed.

I was thrilled when Aaron met Sarah, a wonderful young woman in our group, my future daughter-in-law. It was easy to get to know her and midway through the trip Sarah already felt like my second daughter. Life was good. Due to a set of unexpected circumstances, Aaron and I stayed back from the two-day trip to the open field outside of Rome at Tor Vergata where most of the million and a half young pilgrims would travel for an overnight stay under the stars and a morning papal Mass. Aaron and I rode the buses and trains all over the city, which was almost deserted by then, and had almost exclusive visitation rights to many of the city's ancient ruins since the Romans were at their summer homes and the WYD contingent had left to see the pope. We talked about everything. The choice to stay back blessed us both.

I now had two families: L'Arche, which provided a reasonable facsimile for one, and Aaron and Erica, with whom I was in a parents-can-be-friends-with-their-adult-children transition. It was all gift.

But little did I know that the fleeting thought about a doctor's appointment I needed to keep two days after I returned home would alter forever the way I looked at my life.

I pray that, according to the riches of his glory, he may grant that you may be strengthened in your inner being with power through his Spirit, and that Christ may dwell in your hearts through faith, as you are being rooted and grounded in love.
   (Ephesians 3:16-17)

8
Everything Changes: The Big C
August 31, 2000–October 2000

When I returned to The Arch after Rome, my life was smashed into a gazillion pieces. Within a week I was diagnosed with Stage IV breast cancer. I had a tumor that metastasized through my bloodstream to the lymph nodes and at least one other place in my body. Doctors discovered a 4 mm spot on my lung and one malignant lymph node. The survival rate for Stage IV is around 14 percent. I decided to audition for the group of fourteen who would make it through to the next round.

All the stats were against me. I could easily follow my mother, her sister, and my grandmother to the grave with "the six-month sentence" I remembered hearing about as a child. Most people I knew who had cancer didn't even make it that far. Something had to be done to fix this.

I phoned my children and then my closest friends, to tell them about the cancer. Erica cried and asked if I was going to die. Aaron asked me what I was going to do to get well. My friend Lee asked how he could help. The L'Arche community jumped right in. Our community leader Jo Anne said my role was to "be present" to the core members.

The real possibility of dying in six months caused me to deny my fate by making fun of everything. I made jokes about cancer, death, and the ridiculousness of my surroundings. Death and his companions Pain and Suffering hate satire.

After a month of tests my right breast was removed along with twenty-three lymph nodes. I sang "Thanks for the Mammaries" while being wheeled into surgery. As I went through surgery and eighteen weeks of chemotherapy, assistants, board members, and other friends arranged rides to appointments an hour away, brought dinner, and sent gifts, cards, letters, and e-mails.

My chemo treatment included a ten-page consent form. I happily signed each sheet and drew circles around the words indicating possible side effects of my treatment: "fatal consequences," "respiratory failure," "heart failure," and "death." The complicated dressing gowns required (I'm not kidding) a leaflet and directions (with drawings) posted on the hospital's dressing room wall. I began to appreciate how oncology is so, um, Mary Poppins.

Despite all the fun I was having, I did not choose to be a cancer patient. Sure, it gave me a certain credibility, but I didn't enjoy losing my hair or spending hours each Wednesday having poison dripped into my bloodstream.

It made me nauseated 24/7 and gave me gawd-awful side effects. Blood constantly dripped out of my nose (due to thinning membranes). All my food tasted like metal (due to the chemo). I was compromising my otherwise healthy body by ingesting this crap. I had only a 14 percent chance of getting out of this alive, for God's sake.

In Betty Rollin's story of her bout with breast cancer, she writes: "Death has become more real, so you appreciate not dying."[4] I so totally get this.

The oncology office I grew to know and love was the stage for my personal reality show. The top prize? Life. Prior to each chemo treatment a nurse would insert an L-shaped needle into my chemo port (below my left collarbone) and tape it down. For eighteen weeks they pumped quarts of pre-chemo drugs in me, including Benadryl (Diphenhydramine hydrochloride), to ward off side effects of Taxol (Paclitaxel) and Herceptin (Trastuzumab), the experimental drug I won the right to take in the clinical trial I agreed to in a moment of *why-not*!

One day, a nurse popped in a thirty-minute video about my treatment. Five minutes later, I was asleep. I always wondered if I missed the cartoons.

Every week got weirder, more difficult, and funnier. Black humor, headaches, despair, hope, love, blessings, loneliness, eating, not eating, nausea, weight gain, hair loss, work, anger, acceptance, severe itching, all-over pain, diarrhea, nosebleeds, denial, bargaining, fitful sleep, and insomnia were my buddies.

My hair was falling out and clogging the shower drain, and when I looked in the mirror I saw—yikes!—a scraggly old witch staring back at me. Time to get rid of it all, I said, so I asked Eric if he would do the honors. One Saturday, I invited our community leader Jo Anne over for the event. She took pictures while Eric had at it with the hair clippers. He zipped it all off and the best photo shows how he proudly caught the alien female and held her in the chair with his hand on her bald head. It sure saved me on shampoo and conditioner. A cheap wig from the catalog was good enough for church, and the rest of the time I wore a fleece hat. The times when hot flashes hit, I tossed my cap and let my body heat escape through the skin on my head. Nobody seemed to care. My friend Marion made a flannel pillowcase and lent me her mother's sleeping caps. I never had to shave my legs or underarms. Talk about liberated. I ate anything I wanted and gained forty pounds. My doctors were happy.

When he went ashore, he saw a great crowd; and he had compassion for them and cured their sick.
(Matthew 14:14)

Mass at The Canticle with The Arch Community

October 2000

When I first came to Clinton in 1999, Jean Vanier was visiting. We were at The Canticle, the house of the Clinton Franciscan Sisters. We were invited to Sunday Mass with all the core members. When the priest held up the host and cup and said the words of consecration, "This is my Body, broken for you. This is my blood, poured out for you," I thought about the core members, and I felt grateful and blessed that God gave them to me in this way, as broken bodies.

Exactly one year later, in October of 2000, I was at The Canticle again for Mass with the core members in our house. This time was different. I had just had surgery for breast cancer less than two weeks previous and was still bandaged up and had drainage tubes and bottles hanging from my side. I was going to be starting chemotherapy that week. When the priest said the words of consecration, I heard the words with a different ear. The tables had turned. I felt that my body was broken and blood was being poured out, not for me, but for them. They would be caring for me for a while now, and the line was blurred between who was broken and why. We were broken for each other. This was community. This was the gift of L'Arche.

Now I appeal to you, brothers and sisters, by the name of our Lord Jesus Christ, that all of you be in agreement and that there be no divisions among you, but that you be united in the same mind and the same purpose. (1 Corinthians 1:10)

10 $\mathcal{F}$inding $\mathcal{G}$od in the $\mathcal{F}$lesh

Fall 2000–Spring 2001

During the first six months of my cancer treatment my emotions went for daily rides on a roller coaster. And we're not talking about the old-fashioned wooden ones that made you smile when the ride with grandma was over. We're talking about newfangled monster grippers that some engineer with a death wish created from the evil corner of his warped imagination. My emotions had to be locked into place with steel braces. I could go from hysterical laughter to hellish despair in five seconds. From raging anger to angelic peace in two. Most of my thoughts obsessed over the poison they dripped into my bloodstream each week and how that and the surgery tore at my body, mind, and heart.

Many people, as I did, enter the world of cancer treatment for the first time mostly unaware that they are going to be hauled through the nightmare of a real haunted house. I often found myself sitting in front of my computer,

writing weekly journals, reviewing the past week's experiences, and using every denial technique invented to keep
the demons from busting through the permeable walls of
my sanity and taking over my soul.

However, I found unsought moments of actual grace.
I don't think I asked for them. But God is funny that way.
God always has his way with us, whether or not we have
submitted a requisition form with the details. Suddenly
one day I had an increasing awareness of God incarnate. In
my earlier days as a young Catholic girl attending a very
strict Catholic grade school, I would have been hailed a
heretic for even thinking that the Incarnation could ever
refer to anybody but Jesus. So, hail me a heretic if you will,
but God showed up one day and he had skin. Core members returned with ribbons from Special Olympics saying,
"I won this for you." They joked when I took off my fleece
cap, revealing my bald head. "Put it back!" they'd laugh,
or, "Look, I cut my hair, too."

Damien is a core member with cerebral palsy. He has
no idea, but he healed me at a gathering one night when he
sang "Be Not Afraid." He stood up, his hands twisted and
bent in on themselves, his face scrunched, and sang ". . . and
when you face the power of hell, and death is at your side,
you will see the face of God and live. Be not afraid, I go before you always. Come, follow me. For I will give you rest."
Three days later I was with Damien at Mass. Completely at
random, I flipped the pages to "All will be well, and all will
be well, all manner of things will be well."

Damien's not broken. None of us is. None of us ever was.

During my year of treatment, no core member ever noticed (or at least no one ever said) that I was one breast short, or made disparaging remarks about my hair loss, weight gain, or change in appearance due to the ravaging effects of chemo. It's not that they didn't care; they just didn't pay attention. Persons with the most profound physical and cognitive disabilities live in a culture of separation, rejection, and difference. Some have many doctors, live in wheelchairs, walk with limps, have jerky involuntary movements, communicate with garbled speech, or use communication boards. Their bathroom mirrors reflect faces and bodies my culture doesn't celebrate on covers of celebrity magazines. So, a bald woman, forty pounds overweight with one breast, a red face, and mottled chemo skin, looks just like some of them. I found myself breathing with them more.

On Tuesday nights, I'd tell Bill, Gertie, Marilyn, and Sam that I was going to the doctor. I never said "cancer." Why should I? Many of their friends and family members who had the disease died. If I said I had cancer, they would unnecessarily obsess and worry about my health. I couldn't do that to them.

Bill seemed to be most aware of my situation. He'd always ask, "Doctor? Shot?" and I'd say, "Yes, the doctor will give me a shot." When I returned each week, Bill would point to my chemo port and ask, "Hurt?"

If God is incarnate only in Jesus, then what does it mean that "the Word was made flesh and dwelt among us"? Does it not also mean that living in each of us is the spirit of God, that we are, as our faith teaches us, temples of the Holy Spirit, that when we receive the Eucharist we take God into us and God permeates our beings and we are one with the Divine? When, I might venture to ask, does God disappear from our beings, after our very first encounter with the God of the transubstantiated bread? I do not believe God would ever leave us. The core members in L'Arche have shown me that more than once.

And the Word became flesh and lived among us, and we have seen his glory, the glory as of a father's only son, full of grace and truth. . . . From his fullness we have all received, grace upon grace.

(John 1:14, 16)

11 Marilyn and Her Bath

January 2001

During the winter months that I was undergoing chemo-therapy, I had lost my hair, and I generally wore a fleece hat my high school friend Maria made for me to keep my head warm. I was giving our newest core member, Marilyn, a bath one night and the room was steamy and my head was getting warm. So, I took off my hat and tossed it over in the corner of the room. I suppose at the moment I bared my head perhaps I reminded her of her mother, who had died about a year earlier and also had lost her hair to chemotherapy. Marilyn looked up at me and very gently reached up with her wet, soapy hand and patted my bald head and smiled.

It was the first time in my life I had ever been anointed with soap and water. I didn't want to wipe it off.

> *Are any among you sick? They should call for the elders of the church and have them pray over them, anointing them with oil in the name of the Lord.*
>
> (James 5:14)

12 Head-Painting Party

February 2001

When my chemo ended on Valentine's Day 2001, I decided that I was not going to let this event pass unnoticed. There was no way on God's earth that I would ever want to get this close again to the door of death, and I wasn't sure that on the long shot that the cancer would return that I would want to have chemotherapy be an option.

Chemo was over and my hair would start to grow back. Something had to be done. I arranged a head-painting party to celebrate the end of my treatment. I rounded up all the washable markers we had in the house, put them in a bucket, and on the day after my last chemo treatment we all headed to Arch III for the celebration. We had cake and ice cream, balloons and streamers, music and dancing. I sat on a chair in the middle of the room and invited everyone to grab a marker and have at it.

What fun. The core members were hesitant and didn't know what to do as they probably had never drawn on anybody's bald head before. So, I suggested that assistants come up and show the way. Eric wrote a message, others drew pictures. Then the core members got up, one by one, and started decorating, as if they were making a greeting card on construction paper. Somebody took pictures. Core member Gene dug into my head so hard I thought he was doing brain surgery. Don drew a car. After half an hour, my head was full of lines and colors. Chris made a balloon hat for me and we all got up and danced.

A few days later, when the photos came back from the store, I realized I had used old markers and the colors were faint. This was a once-in-a-lifetime chance, and I didn't want to blow it. My hair would start growing back in a couple weeks, and so I invited everyone back for a second party. I bought new markers, and the core members were even more eager to leave their marks. We had an even bigger celebration. We kicked death out the back door.

Listen, I will tell you a mystery! We will not all die, but we will all be changed, in a moment, in the twinkling of an eye, at the last trumpet. For the trumpet will sound, and the dead will be raised imperishable, and we will be changed. . . . When this perishable

body puts on imperishability, and this mortal body puts on immortality, then the saying that is written will be fulfilled:

"Death has been swallowed up in victory."
"Where, O death, is your victory?
Where, O death, is your sting?"
(1 Corinthians 15:51-52, 54-55)

13 Marilyn and Mark: Christmas Stories

December 2001

Marilyn and Mark are core members who are about fifty years old. Both exhibit many behaviors that resemble a four-year-old. Both have the innocence of a child in their voices and actions.

It was Christmas and I asked Marilyn what the name of the donkey was that her patron saint rode when she was pregnant with Jesus. She thought a second, looked up at me, and said with a light and sweet voice, "Thunderbolt."

Later, Mark came downstairs and said, "I had a dream last night." I couldn't wait to hear it. You never know what kind of sugar plums are dancing around in this man's head this time of year. I asked, "What did you dream about?" and he said, "Rudolph." I asked, "As in 'Rudolph the Red Nosed Reindeer'?" He nodded. I asked him what happened. He paused briefly, looked down, and, in a very serious, no-nonsense, and very sad voice reported, "Burl Ives killed him."

Truly I tell you, unless you change and become like children, you will never enter the kingdom of heaven.
(Matthew 18:3)

14 Good Friday and Bill

March 2002

It was Good Friday. We were all at church for services. It came time for the veneration of the cross and I wasn't sure if Bill remembered what to do, but I knew that he could follow simple directions. He won't do something if he doesn't know what he's supposed to do, so I leaned over and whispered, "Just do what everybody else does. You can kiss the cross or just touch it." He nodded, and I knew he would be all right. We waited in line.

Father Smith was holding the cross. Bill likes Father Smith and considers him his "pal." We quietly walked up to the cross and Bill stepped ahead of me. He knelt down and kissed the cross. Then he stood up and reached over and shook Father Smith's hand. Father Smith looked up and smiled.

Afterward, I wondered how one should approach a person who is carrying a cross. Perhaps if I shook the person's hand who was carrying a cross, focusing on the person and not the cross, it might just be a little more human, a little more compassionate, a little more loving than merely touching the dead wood.

They compelled a passer-by, who was coming in from the country, to carry his cross; it was Simon of Cyrene, the father of Alexander and Rufus.
(Mark 15:21)

15 My Mother's Birthday and that Damn Can of Pop

Date of incident: May 8, 2002 (Written November 2007)

One sunny and peaceful Wednesday morning five years ago, on the day I was celebrating my deceased mother's birthday—May 8, 2002—something so horrible happened, I still have a hard time speaking about it.

The morning started well. At breakfast, I mentioned that my mother would have been ninety-four years old that day. I asked the core members what they knew about their mothers. All but Sam's had gone to heaven. Only Bill did not know his mom's name. Sam asked me my mother's name and I said, "Isabelle." He said, "That's nice." Even though I knew, I asked him his mom's name. He told me. Then I asked him what he wanted to get her for Mother's Day that coming Sunday, and he said, "A necklace." So I asked, "Cross or heart?" He said, "Cross." Sam loves crosses, especially large and heavy ones.

Despite the years of challenges I'd had with him, almost from the moment I arrived at The Arch, that morning began wonderfully. We were having a real, human, pleasant conversation. We were talking about our moms. I felt surprisingly connected and since it was my mom's birthday, I felt that God's grace had come upon us. I felt blessed. Perhaps God had answered my prayer and Sam and I could relate more peacefully from now on.

I had no idea that within only a few minutes the morning would turn very ugly. I went upstairs to help another core member find a shirt, and when I came back Sam was walking up from the basement with his lunch box in his hand. Odd, I thought, so I asked what he was doing, and with a sheepish grin on his face he said, "Nothing." I had a gut feeling he took something and put it into his lunch box, so asked him to let me see what he had in there, and he opened it and showed me a can of pop he had taken from the basement.

What happened next has been burned into my memory with the permanence of a branding iron. I looked at the can of pop, and realizing that he took something that wasn't his, I immediately felt betrayed. But the betrayal wasn't because he had taken something. It was because five minutes earlier the two of us had somehow reconciled our differences. Or so I thought. Sam and I had talked calmly, without his usual bragging, without his usual loud voice, about our mothers. It was the first time in over two and a half years that he and I connected, almost—almost— as peers, at least on some emotional level. Something we could build on. The disappointment, the perception of it being a betrayal of this new relationship, was greater than I would have expected.

I reacted. I looked down at the floor, shook my head, and in a forced whisper, said one word: "Dammit." Then I looked up into the face of a man who was suddenly afraid. The earth stopped moving beneath our feet. Apparently for both of us. I stood there silently. He held out his hand with the can of pop. That should have been the end of it for now. I didn't think he would get violent. I had no apprehension, no fear of saying directly, "You took something that was not yours. You're in trouble." I took the can from his hand. He was a frightened man, backed into a corner. Immediately I found out what it feels like to be a victim of violence. He pointed his finger at me and jabbed me in the face. I held up my hands to protect myself and said, "Sam, don't hit me. I want you to go to your room and calm down." He said, "You swore." I said, "I'm sorry." I let down my guard. I could not explain anything to him at this point. Neither of us were in the same space as we were when we were sitting at the table.

Then he punched me in the mouth. I held up my hands again and repeated, "Sam, don't hit me. I want you to go to your room and calm down." He did not stop. He punched me in the face three more times. Each time I asked him to go to his room. Blood ran from the cuts inside my mouth and on my cheek. When I turned away, he kicked me in the back, rabbit-punched me in the side, and pushed me out of the way so he could run out the door.

No other assistants were in the house that morning, but several core members were. They stood there and watched, helpless to do more than witness the attack. After it was over, I reached for the phone and dialed our director. Then I sat on the bench with my head down. I remember sobbing. I felt hands on my shoulders and arms wrapped around me. I raised my head to find the other core members standing over me, hugging me and holding on to me. One brushed her hand on my cheek. They said nothing. I looked up and whispered, "Thank you."

Although the only permanent physical scar is a white line alongside my nose from where Sam jabbed me with his fingernail, it has taken me all these years to be able to speak about the event without getting angry. No matter how much I say I believe that when you are doing God's work God will provide, that morning I didn't feel that God provided anything. I was not rescued from the attack. No masked and red-caped superhero appeared to save me from that first punch. No lifeboat pulled up and threw me a life preserver.

However alone I felt, however much I felt I was out there without anyone or anything to save me, I know now that I was never abandoned. A small group of men and women with mental retardation appeared to me and tended to my emotional wounds with their silent and gentle touch.

When God brought me to this ark, I never thought I would face violence. The core members I first met seemed to be calm and happy. But my life in L'Arche teaches me that we are so much more the same than we are different, regardless of our cognitive abilities. If we have emotions at all, we are capable of violence. And given the right conditions, blind rage can explode from anywhere, anytime.

The shock of being beaten up blinded me from any possible response other than anger and retribution. The interplay of the morning gave me a false sense of security, and I could not comprehend the massive dynamics that were taking place between us. I falsely judged the situation and my history and my feelings unconsciously clouded my decisions.

We walk into every moment of our lives carrying the entire history of our experiences. Written on our psyches are all of our reactions, emotions, feelings, memories, thoughts, judgments, expectations, hopes, and all of the interactions we have ever had, positive, negative, and neutral. I came to the morning of May 8, 2002, with all of that. So did Sam.

After I was attacked, I was in shock. I was in pain. I took the whole thing personally and the view I took was that Sam hurt me and I probably needed to forgive him. The word stalked me, haunted me. Forgiveness. To hell with it. This man beat me up and it hurt, and my privacy along with my body were attacked. I will never condone his actions. We have the right to be safe and persons with disabilities must be accountable for their actions. So, my thoughts and actions went the route of trying to fix the problem. I desperately wanted him to be on prescription medication to control his violent outbursts. I believed that cognitive therapy doesn't generally work and even when there is a chance it will, it often requires many years of intense work to overcome long histories of violent tendencies and behaviors.

But that's not what this whole thing was really about. The question was whether I would ever be able to forgive him. It's that simple. I said, "No, I would not."

I once read a definition that also haunted me: "Forgiveness is abandoning all hope of ever having had a better past." What does that mean? Forget it. It's over. You can't relive the past. Use what happened as a textbook and learn from it. Let your physical and/or emotional scars be reminders of a chapter, or a paragraph, in your story. Move on. We are the sum of our experiences and we learn the most from our worst ones.

My response? Bullshit.

I bought a greeting card once that showed a frightening drawing on the front of a very traumatized cat cowering up on a fence in a dark alley with several mean-looking dogs barking at it from the ground. The caption on the front said: "We grow and learn the most in our lives from our most difficult experiences." On the inside, it read: "I hate it that it works like that."

That's exactly how I felt. Don't preach at me. Don't tell me crap about how I am supposed to feel. I went through cancer and then somebody beat me up and I'm just supposed to forgive this man? No. I can't and I won't.

I remember reading something by Ram Dass, the controversial '60s guru and friend of Timothy Leary. He said that people are spiritually fortunate when they experience trauma because it affords them opportunities to grow. He added that we should never look for misfortune or whip ourselves with knotted ropes, but rather see whatever happens to us as a gift rather than a curse.

My late cousin Louie also said that about my life and work in L'Arche. Shortly before he died from cancer, we spoke on the phone. Louie said that I would be gaining a lot of spiritual ground in L'Arche because it was a holy place to serve God. I wonder if he knew that I was unable to forgive Sam for the beating.

I could never tell Louie what I really thought about his idea. I respected him and loved him. The gifts of service and pain, he said, were probably not on our must-have lists, and surely nobody in their right mind would ask Santa for a box of suffering to appear under the tree on Christmas morning. But he felt that I was "lucky" to be here because I would be growing by leaps and bounds spiritually.

Louie never preached at me. He never spoke above me, even though he had a PhD in entomology and had studied spiritual practices all over the world in his work-related travels to rid native forests of crop-killing pests. Louie was funny and empathetic, and he eased my pain. A little.

In the years since the attack, I have been confronted by L'Arche assistants and people on The Arch board and elsewhere about whether I was able, ready, and/or willing to forgive the people at The Arch who have hurt me. The beating I've described hasn't been the only time I was hit. Other core members have kicked and hit me when they have been out of control, and for some reason unknown to me then, I happened to be in the way.

I was not ready to forgive anybody for hurting me.

But Louie's words and his love were good. And true. Life is a dance, and I have discovered that God is always present, particularly on the deck of this ark and perhaps even more especially in the hold where it's dark, damp, and dank.

Our founder Jean Vanier has also spoken of forgiveness: "The Greek word for forgiveness is *asphesis*, which means to liberate, to release from bondage; it means the remission of debt, guilt, and punishment. It is used when the prison door is opened and the prisoner can go free."[5]

I did not feel free. Lack of forgiveness continued to enslave me. This freedom must be a process of the heart.

I attended a national Catholic conference on peace and justice not long after the attack and went to a breakout session by a woman whose pregnant sister and brother-in-law were brutally murdered in their home by a neighbor boy, a mentally ill teenager. She said that she simply made a choice to forgive this young man. She did not condone his behavior, but realized that forgiveness was a way to let go of the emotional and psychic pain she suffered after those grisly deaths. For her, it was an intellectual choice. Her healing continued as she began a foundation in memory of her sister's family and by giving talks on forgiveness anywhere she is welcome.

It's been years since Sam beat me up. I have listened to the people who spoke of forgiveness. Nobody can tell me how I should respond or when. There is no right way to forgive and no timeline.

I met a woman at a centering prayer retreat in New York years ago who spoke calmly of the day she was raped and beaten in her apartment by a stranger. She said she chose to not let him control her life, and so she forgave him so that she could live peacefully again. She said rationally that the incident happened and it became part of her life story, but she was not going to hang on to it and let it continue to hurt her. She, too, did not condone her attacker's behavior. She simply regained control of her life and cognitively let it go.

Was it really that easy? I don't know. But if I want something to happen, why can't I trust God to help me let it happen?

I'm on the path to forgiveness. Perhaps one day I will look behind me and realize that the heavy bag filled with the rocks of hurt and anger I've been dragging is finally empty. Meanwhile, I try to find my way.

I began to reason that the man who hurt me was likely abused while institutionalized as a young man and he had learned to react that way to situations where he felt threatened or trapped. I further reasoned that he had misunderstood and misinterpreted the violence he saw on TV and in movies as being real ways to handle conflict, and so he learned to punch, jab, and kick in order to protect himself, or simply to win. He learned that to be a man it was important to be physically strong, but more importantly it was his fear that caused him to respond with physical violence when he thought that he was going to be hurt or punished. His fear of the unknown—in this case, unknown consequences for taking the can of pop—caused a gut-induced, almost evolutionary response.

During this time of processing, The Arch's community leader asked me if I had looked at my own violence in order to help me forgive this man so I could move on and be a better assistant in this L'Arche community. I immediately became defensive. She continued anyway. We all have violence within us, she said. Some is exhibited verbally. We are mean and rude to others. She admitted that she realized once when she was short with somebody that it was a violent act. I believe now that she was right. Violence disturbs the peace. It breaks the connection to love and compassion. Or it bends it for a while.

I asked myself what brought this violence into my life, why I was violated, why my peace was disturbed. I wonder if it's so I can experience God in the pursuit of forgiveness, so that I can really grow spiritually and learn more about compassion. Perhaps.

Whether the violence came to me because it entered through a crack in my spirit or because I simply needed to learn how to truly forgive is unimportant. I think what matters is whether I am now more aware of the cracks, whether I have learned how to forgive, and if God was present in the process.

I believe God has been present. "To forgive is to break down the walls of hostility that separate us, and to bring each other out of the anguish of loneliness, fear, and chaos into communion and oneness," Vanier says at the end of his chapter on forgiveness.[6]

Surely God was in the core members who huddled around me and offered solace and comfort that morning. God was in my attempt to understand the man who attacked me. God was in my awareness that I am able to live in moments of violence and never feel abandoned. God was in my heart as I admitted that violence isn't always physical and I am guilty of violating the peace as well. But most of all, for this moment, God is always here. God never abandons me. Communion is possible after all.

Bear with one another and, if anyone has a complaint against another, forgive each other; just as the Lord has forgiven you, so you also must forgive.
(Colossians 3:13)

16 *The Night of the Incident*

October 2002

One Friday night Bruce, a core member in my house, threatened to kill me as he came toward me with his shaver in his hand. I ran up the stairs as Bruce stood at the bottom of the steps threatening my life. I asked Gene to get the phone. I called our director who called the police. It felt like forever before they arrived. Meanwhile Bruce continued shaking his razor at me, calling me obscene names and screaming at me, "I'll kill you, bitch!" I had no idea if he was going to attack me or anyone else in the house. I was the only assistant in the house at the time.

Mark and Vincent were also in the house. Mark is a core member who exhibits some signs of autism and has behaviors which resemble a four-year-old even though he is in his forties. Vincent has Down syndrome, is more serious by nature, and rarely speaks except in a soft, indecipherable mumble.

When the police and our director finally arrived, they took Bruce into the dining room and I found myself in the living room, trembling from fear and shock. Vincent quietly walked over to me and put his arms around me. Then he let go and put one arm around my waist and led me to the couch where he made me sit down. I was such a jumbled mess that I just did what he wanted. He sat down next to me and reached for my hand and held it. I glanced over at him and whispered, "Thank you." He nodded, smiled, and kept holding my hand for a few minutes until I told him I was okay.

After about twenty minutes the police took Bruce away. I sensed a high level of anxiety in the house and it was upsetting Mark, who is very sensitive to his surroundings. He also knew I was upset, and so he kept saying, "Kathy, be happy." I told him I was all right. I'm sure he knew I was lying. He said it again. "Kathy, be happy." I repeated, "Mark, I'm fine. Let's go pray." So, we sat down in the living room, lit some candles, and put on some soft music. But Mark saw through my attempt to be calm. He kept saying, "Kathy, be happy. Be happy, Kathy." And then he said, "Jesus, make Kathy happy." I looked at his face. I said, "Mark, are you okay?" He said, "Jesus make happy." He wanted to feel safe and make the problems go away, so he kept repeating "Jesus make happy" over and over, trying to bring calm to himself, the other core members, and me.

Then he said something he had never said before and which I have not heard him say since. Mark, the man who does not like to be touched and seldom touches others, the man who acts more like a toddler than an adult, reached over to me, reassuringly touched my hand, and said in a very mature and calm voice, "Kathy, I'm glad you're here."

Blessed are those who mourn, for they will be comforted. (Matthew 5:4)

17 Just Another Sunday Morning

March 2003

It was a Sunday, a day we all can sleep in. But at six a.m. I heard loud noises—doors opening and closing. Those stupid automatic door closers on their bedroom doors. I hated them even more that day. Every ten minutes or so, I'd hear a series of opening, closing, opening, closing, opening, closing. But it was more like soft slamming because of the closers. I heard footsteps with shoes. I heard drawers opening and closing downstairs in the kitchen. People walking up and down the staircase. Noises would start then stop. I first thought that the core members were getting up and going to the bathroom. I didn't worry about anybody getting in trouble. So, at seven thirty, I got up to take a shower and didn't see or hear anybody. Good, they went back to bed, I thought.

At eight a.m., when I emerged from the bathroom, prepared to start people moving for the day, Gene was outside

his room asking if it was time to get up. I said, "Yes." It appeared two other core members were already up and probably dressed.

I went downstairs to find Vincent sitting on a chair in the living room and Bruce in the dining room—both dressed and ready for church. Dishes were put away and the garbage cans were emptied. For some unknown reason, I was angry. Perhaps it was because some core members got up in the middle of the night and got ready for the day and disturbed the people who were sleeping. We had told them they needed to stay in their rooms until an assistant comes to get them because their noises take away the others' right to sleep. Both Vincent and Bruce habitually got up during the middle of the night, got dressed, and came downstairs. Of course they'd be tired by suppertime and then we would have to deal with that issue.

I told Vincent that I was not happy that he got up so early, because he made a lot of noise that woke everybody else up, especially when he was putting away the dishes downstairs. I said the same thing to Bruce, who liked to get up and empty all the wastebaskets in the house.

Then it started. Bruce wouldn't stop apologizing. "I'm sorry I got up early. I will stay in bed next time," he said over and over, all morning, about every ten minutes. My patience was wearing thin. I didn't want to hear any more from him. His apologies started to annoy me. I wanted to say, "It's over already, I talked to you and we agreed you would not do that again and now let's get on with the day."

But it didn't matter. He kept apologizing and saying he was sorry—on and on and on and on.

I tried to ignore Bruce as I gave Vincent his morning meds. Vincent had not said a word all morning. He usually doesn't talk much anyway, and when he does it's in a mumbled whisper. I wasn't even looking at him since I was still upset with his getting up so early. I sat there and I looked up only enough to administer his meds. Vincent was silent. He kept his head down most of the time, too. Then I heard him whisper. Two syllables were all I could make out. I knew the word immediately, but I wanted him to say it so I could see his face. So I asked him, "What did you say?" I looked right at him. He whispered in the smallest voice, "Sorry."

I stopped. I looked up and into his eyes and nodded. He was sorry. He never said another word about it. It was over. He did something that upset the house and he apologized. Meanwhile, Bruce continued telling me over and over that he did wrong and that he was sorry. Over and over, every few minutes.

I looked back on this later and wondered which of these two men my own behavior and attitude resemble. Of course, I wanted to say Vincent, but the truth is Bruce. I want to make things right. I want to make sure the person I offended isn't upset anymore. I want to keep saying "I'm sorry." But Vincent had to say it only once. He said it quietly. He was sincere. The look on his face and the tone of his voice were sufficient.

When Jesus saw their faith, he said to the paralytic,
"Son, your sins are forgiven." (Mark 2:5)

18 Batman and the Bat

April 2003

I came back from my time away at nine a.m. one Tuesday and saw a purple towel in front of the basement door. Katey, the other assistant at Arch III, said we had a bat in the house. She said that she had taken an old pizza box downstairs and was swinging it at the creature. I told her I'd rather catch it and let it go than kill it, especially with a sacred pizza box, for heaven's sake! I decided, as the know-it-all house coordinator, to take measures into my own hands.

But never having dealt with the likes of a bat before, I wondered how I would catch one. Do they bite? Would it try to escape and hide somewhere only to emerge at night flying around my room? Would I get rabies? Or worse yet, nightmares?

I called Eric. He was the house coordinator at Arch I where I lived when I arrived at The Arch. I knew he had a special, secret, symbiotic relationship with all living beings.

Plus, he was always glad to help me out. His normal routine for catching bats is this: He would arrive armed with a colander and a giant salad bowl. He would ask the whereabouts of the creature in question. He would walk up to the bat and calmly speak to it. Then he would take the colander and gently coax it inside. He would cover it with the bowl and carry it outside. He would drive to the park five miles away to let it escape into the wilds so it wouldn't try to return to the house. How like St. Francis he was. Or Doctor Dolittle.

However, St. Eric Francis Dolittle was on vacation that week. The bat was still in the basement. I didn't have a plan B, so I took my chances and waited for something miraculous to happen.

The bat apparently hid in the basement, waiting for Eric to return from vacation. When he did, he came right over and rescued me from the terrors of having a nocturnal rabies-carrying swooping/flying creature in my house.

I'm such a chicken.

Then the king was exceedingly glad and commanded that Daniel be taken up out of the den. So Daniel was taken up out of the den, and no kind of harm was found on him, because he had trusted in his God. (Daniel 6:23)

19 Vincent and the Angel's Message

June 2004

One evening I was sitting with Vincent at the dining room table. The four other core members had already gone up to bed. I thought this would be my chance to find out if Vincent was the angel I always suspected, because I figured that if he really *was* an angel, he would tell me. So, with echoes of the TV show *Touched by an Angel* resounding in my head, I leaned over to Vincent, looked him square in the eye, and asked, "Vincent, are you really an angel?"

He looked at me with no expression other than confidence on his face and said, "Yeah." I was, let's say, without a doubt, very excited. Wanting more than anything to have firsthand contact with a real angel, I needed to know if he had any messages for me. I believe that angels are truly God's messengers.

I said, "Vincent, do you have any messages for me from God?" He looked at me seriously and in a quiet voice whispered, "Yeah." Oh brother, I'm on a roll now. I was getting really pumped. I couldn't wait to find out what God had to tell me. So, I leaned over closer to him and said, "Ok, so you're an angel, right? So, what's God's message for me?" Vincent slowly turned around, lifted his hand, pointed into the kitchen, and said softly, "Cake."

"Wait, wait, did I hear that right? You said, 'Cake'?! That was it? The message God wanted me to hear was 'Cake'?" Vincent looked at me, and with a voice determined to get a second dessert, he said, "Yeah!"

I was crushed. "Vincent, do you mean to tell me that God told you to tell me to give you some cake?"

Again, with an even more determined voice, he said, "Yeeaaahhh!"

I learned my lesson. I received my message: God sends angels in God's time, not mine, and more importantly, not to play games with nosy, smart alecks like me.

The angel replied, "I am Gabriel. I stand in the presence of God, and I have been sent to speak to you and to bring you this good news." (Luke 1:19)

20 Vincent and Gene at Danny's Wake

August 2004

Two days after Danny died from a heart attack, Vincent and Gene wanted to go to his wake. Danny was a forty-four-year-old man they knew from Skyline workshop who also had Down syndrome. Vincent and Gene put on their Sunday clothes, and we drove to the funeral home to pay our last respects. We walked into the building and signed our names in the guest book and then walked up to the casket where Danny was lying. Vincent stood there, looked at Danny's face, and without any sense of self-consciousness or hesitation gently placed his right hand on Danny's folded hands. I watched Vincent standing at the side of the casket, head bent forward, looking for a long, long time into Danny's unmoving face.

After several minutes, Vincent carefully removed his hand from Danny's, took a step back, and held his own hands up. He held them together, making a triangle of his index fingers and thumbs, and lifted his hands in reverence toward Danny's body. I noticed the triangle, the Trinity, the sign of blessing Vincent was making for his friend. Then Gene and I joined Vincent to say our last good-byes to their friend.

I stood between them, putting my arms around their shoulders, and asked if they wanted to say a prayer for Danny. They nodded. We stood in silence a few seconds and then Gene started. "Our Father . . ." he said, and Vincent and I continued, "Who art in heaven. . . ." The three of us quietly said the Lord's Prayer for Danny.

I took my arms away from Vincent and Gene. Vincent stepped closer to the casket, gently placed his left hand a few inches over Danny's chest, and, in sign language, made the universal sign for "I love you."

We walked out of the funeral home and passed the hearse parked on the street. We talked about how this car would take Danny to the cemetery and that he was going to heaven. Neither Vincent nor Gene said a word.

Later, at home, I looked out the window and noticed the funeral procession passing by our house, so I said to the core members, "There goes Danny in the hearse on his way to the cemetery."

Vincent looked up at the window and raised his right hand and held it up for a few seconds toward the street as the cars went past and silently said his last good-bye.

Do not let your hearts be troubled. Believe in God, believe also in me. In my Father's house there are many dwelling places. If it were not so, would I have told you that I go to prepare a place for you? And if I go and prepare a place for you, I will come again and will take you to myself, so that where I am, there you may be also. (John 14:1-3)

21 The Blood on Don's Face

November 2005

The phone rang one night. It was Kevin, a core member who lives in the apartment building next door and is roommates with another core member, Don. "Don's bleeding," he said into the phone.

My God, Don's bleeding?! Our part-time assistant Sister Luke had already left for home and I was the only assistant in the house.

"What happened?" I asked.

"I don't know," Kevin said.

"Where is he bleeding?" I asked.

"His face," Kevin replied.

"His face is bleeding?" I asked. "Let me talk to Don."

Don got on the phone. "Hello," he said in a calm and serious voice.

"Don, are you bleeding?" I asked.

"I think so," he said, again in a calm voice.

"Where are you bleeding?" I wanted to know.

"Here," he said. Like I could see him over the phone.

"What part of your body is bleeding?" I asked.

"I don't know," Don said.

"Is it your face? Is your face bleeding? Do you need help?" I asked, trying to figure out what was wrong.

"Yes, I think so," Don replied.

"Are you able to come over here?" I asked.

"Yes," he said.

"Well, Don," I said, "Then come on over and let me see."

Don walked into the house a minute later. I looked at his face and saw a lot of dried blood on his nose.

"What happened to you?" I asked, trying to get answers to the mystery.

"I think I opened the freezer door or something," he said.

"And you banged your nose into the door? Let me look at that," I said.

It looked like a big scar with a pile of scabby, dried blood on it. So I said, "Come here and sit down. Let's wash it off."

I took a wet tissue and gently rubbed Don's nose. The blood finally came off. Then I looked at the tissue and then back at Don's nose where there was no more blood.

"Don," I said. "This isn't blood."

"It's not?" he said, surprised.

"No, Don," I said. "It's chocolate. You got chocolate on your nose when you opened the freezer."

"Oops," he said, smiling. Then he stretched out his big arms, reached up, and gave me a hug.

We both smiled.

"Bye Don, have a good evening," I said.

"Bye Kathy," he said as he walked out of the house and back to his apartment.

Blessed are the pure in heart, for they will see God.
(Matthew 5:8)

22 Vicar Randy Thinks He's a Prophet

January 28, 2007

Jean Vanier writes about sin:

> I discovered something which I had never confronted
> before, that there were immense forces of darkness and
> hatred within my own heart. At particular moments of
> fatigue or stress, I saw forces of hate rising up inside
> me, and the capacity to hurt someone who was weak
> and was provoking me! That, I think, was what caused
> me the most pain: to discover who I really am, and to
> realize that maybe I did not want to know who I really
> was! I did not want to admit all the garbage inside
> me. And then I had to decide whether I would just
> continue to pretend that I was okay and throw myself
> into hyperactivity, projects where I could forget all the
> garbage and prove to others how good I was. Elitism is

the sickness of us all. We all want to be on the winning team. That is the heart of apartheid and every form of racism. The important thing is to become conscious of those forces in us and to work at being liberated from them and to discover that the worst enemy is inside our own hearts not outside![7]

It was Sunday morning and I felt like hell.

I was sitting with all five core members from my house in the third pew on the right side at St. Paul's Lutheran Church. I go there on Sundays because that's where all the core members from my house are members. The service was strange that day and I doubt that many Catholic churches, at least the ones I've been to in recent years, would ever have allowed what happened that morning to happen.

This is not, however, a story about how Pastor Elizabeth and Vicar Randy and the parish council used their creativity to tell parishioners how to stop taking heat, Sunday bulletins, and the organist for granted. We didn't get bulletins that morning so we were unable to follow the readings and the order of the service or to know what songs to sing or what was going on that week in the parish. Vicar Randy said they were going to turn down the heat that morning, but it was so cold outside that the furnace was already cranking at high gear just to keep up. So, although they wanted to teach us a lesson, they also didn't want us to freeze and never come back. It was a good choice. The other would have been counterproductive. Okay, so far I was with them.

The only music was from a piano. The choir stayed home and so we spoke rather than sang the service. Communion was by intinction (to save on wine) instead of from those miniature shot glasses. Really, we were suffering, and Vicar Randy and Pastor Elizabeth read from scripts that said it could always be like this if we didn't contribute $1,000 a month to keep ourselves in heat, bulletins, the choir, and wine.

I'll give them credit for trying to make a point. I was on the verge of telling them that many Catholic churches manage on bare-bones budgets, too, but I didn't because I like Elizabeth and Randy too much to throw stones.

So, there I was sitting in the third pew, minding my own business, and frankly feeling rather crabby about life. I don't like our new work schedule, and I was feeling sorry for myself about everything. The stupid weather is too cold. I'm not in Wisconsin where Aaron and Sarah are about to have my first grandchild, Isaac. I'm getting older and don't know what I want to do when I grow up yet, for God's sake.

Mark sat next to me, his green Lutheran hymnal open on his lap. Didn't he know we weren't using the Lutheran hymnal this morning? There weren't any bulletins this morning for him to take home and stash in his sacred drawer alongside all the other crap he brings home. It's a Junk Drawer. Pack Rats like us grew up with the family Junk Drawer. The Pack Rat Creed is: "Don't throw that away because you never know when you might need it. The day you throw it out, that's when you will need it."

So, here I was, sitting in the third pew at church, feeling crabby, hungry, frustrated, and cold. Mark turned to me, reached out his hand, and said, "I like you, Kathy."

Now I felt guilty for feeling crabby. It was time for the sermon. Vicar Randy is interning at St. Paul's. He's from Texas but claims he doesn't have a Texas drawl, y'all. He does make me laugh sometimes, even when I'm feeling crabby. He said the gospel was from "Luke, chapter 4, verses 21 through 30." He said it twice, and then was interrupted by Pastor Elizabeth who asked how people were going to follow along if they didn't have their bulletins, so, with a tiny smile, Randy said, "If y'all (no accent, eh, Randy?) could just turn to that passage in your Bibles . . ." and his voice trailed off. Even Catholics know that ELCA Lutherans don't carry Bibles to church. So, on cue, the altar server went over and picked up a three-by-four-foot poster board with a summary of the gospel printed with a wide black permanent marker. He paraded that thing up and down the center aisle while we all smiled and laughed at the silliness of it all. But let's not forget the point: don't take church bulletins for granted. Or the heat. Or the organist. Or wine. Or you will live to regret it.

Now I felt cavalier. Catholics like me, after all, don't need bulletins to follow the readings. We're supposed to listen to the reader telling us a story. We like pianos, and we keep our coats on in church because Father can't afford to heat the place just for a couple of hours on a Sunday morning. How arrogant I suddenly became!

Vicar Randy started reading and we listened. It was something about Jesus being a prophet. The one where a prophet is not welcome in his own town. So, Randy told us that if we were really Christians, we'd walk WITH Jesus and not merely NEXT TO him. For the next twenty minutes I sat there, cold, hungry, frustrated, crabby, and arrogant, listening to Randy dare to tell us that he was going to make us uncomfortable with what he was about to say next. And he'd shout the words "with" and "next to" just for Texas-size emphasis.

Bring it on. I was all ears. St. Paul's was once a well-to-do parish, he said. People around me bristled. He continued: "We [meaning 'you'] come to church to be fed, and then we [meaning 'you'] go home and watch football."

Vicar Randy was on a roll. Nobody was throwing Lutheran hot dishes yet, so he said he was going to make us even more uncomfortable. Then he hit us with the big one and we (meaning "you") were prepared. "We aren't walking WITH Jesus," he said. "We're just walking NEXT TO Jesus." From his tone we guessed that wasn't good.

To walk WITH Jesus means walking in his shoes, doing what he did, living the acts of mercy, living the Beatitudes, and living the virtues, not just memorizing them from the Bible. Walking WITH Jesus meant giving up everything and turning our (meaning "your") life over to Christ and following him in every way. We don't do that, Randy said, we just walk NEXT TO Jesus, chitchatting with him, putting pictures of him in our homes and churches, saying prescribed prayers, tossing a little money into the collection plate on Sunday so the church can operate, sending a missionary or two to live in some developing country. "But what are we doing," Randy asked, "to really walk WITH Jesus?"

The bristling stopped. We were stunned into silence.

So, there I sat, in the third pew, and Vicar Randy, with all his humor, cleverness, and theatrics, was working very hard this morning at being that guy who wasn't going to be accepted in his own town. He said he came that morning to make us really uncomfortable. I was surprised and a little embarrassed at how I was beginning to feel.

Randy, you devil. You obviously aren't talking to me. I live in a L'Arche community. I already walk WITH Jesus. I turned my life over to him seven and a half years ago when I came here, when I gave away most of my stuff to the Hmong community in Green Bay to live and work with persons with disabilities. I was doing exactly what God asked and, by God, I was a Christian.

How right on top of things I felt. I didn't feel nearly as guilty as the people around me probably did. I glanced over at the five core members sitting around me and thought, "I've got my ticket to heaven. I'm a L'Arche assistant. It's the ultimate sacrifice. Randy definitely is not talking to me."

Randy does not have the guts to face me and ask—no, demand—that I give it all up—again—and walk WITH Jesus. He wouldn't dare tell me that I was merely walking

NEXT TO Jesus and that I wasn't a real Christian. I am exempt because I *am* a real Christian. Not only am I serving the poor, I am living with them and caring for them 24/7. I sat up straighter, gave myself a smug little smile, and felt like I did when I was in first grade and Sister selected me to be Our Lady of Fatima for the school play. I had my ticket to heaven in my hand.

I left church and told Randy on my way out that I enjoyed his humor and thought he did a great job with the sermon. I could finally go home.

Later that evening we all gathered back at St. Paul's for the monthly community meal in the church's fellowship hall. The five core members in my house plus another assistant and I walked downstairs into the basement, hung up our coats, and found our way to an empty table. I've been to only one of these meals because I'm normally gone on Sunday evenings. But since I was around that day, I went. It's one of those free meals for anybody, but "anybody" really means people who are homeless, who have no real money, who live in group homes or shelters or low-income housing or live alone on a very fixed income and may also be elderly, very poor, and uneducated.

So, there I was, sitting smugly in a room with all the faces of a poor Jesus, all the smells of an unwashed Jesus, all the brokenness of a beaten Jesus, all the loneliness of a rejected Jesus. Trying very hard not to be one of those "anybodies." The woman ahead of me in line smelled as if she hadn't taken a bath in a week, and I guessed she'd worn that same old ragged blue sweatshirt and sweatpants for at least as long. The old man at the table next to ours hadn't washed or cut his hair in months, hadn't shaved or changed his clothes either, hadn't been to the dentist—and I'm guessing the doctor—in many years. The man at the piano, who had to be asked to stop playing so we could say Grace, probably struggled to keep food in his cupboard and friends at his table. The woman who stopped by for a carryout didn't have a job and her fiancé told her he didn't want to get married and she struggled with personal demons she may never face.

I don't walk WITH Jesus if I don't talk to these people, offer to cook for them and befriend them. I don't walk WITH Jesus if the way I look at them is judgmental and critical. I don't walk WITH Jesus if I think that living in a L'Arche community is enough, if I don't see the face of Jesus in the people I live with all the time, if I am crabby because I have to work an extra twenty-four hours with the persons I came here to serve. I don't walk WITH Jesus if all I'm thinking about is my own comfort, if I am not patient with the persons I live with, the persons with disabilities whose job it is to keep exposing the face of Jesus to me until I finally surrender. Surreptitiously surrender.

So, there I sat, at that round table in the basement of St. Paul's, looking at, listening to, and smelling the bodies of Christ, feeling very humbled for feeling very smug that morning as I sat in the third pew of the church upstairs where I was sitting NEXT TO Jesus instead of WITH Jesus.

I saw Randy over by the food table. I walked up to him with my head down. I told him his sermon struck a nerve. He explained that the evangelist Billy Graham once said that most of us approach Christianity like an inoculation: we get vaccinated with a little dose and then never catch it again. I said I understood.

The prophet Randy did his job. He made me feel uncomfortable. I did not welcome his words into my life. I rejected him as I would a rotten potato. As we always reject those who come to speak the truth we can't bear to hear.

I doubted everything our Lutheran prophet said and would not believe that his words held any truth until I saw the nail prints in the dirty hands of the poor and put my finger into the gaping wound of their brokenness.

Oh dear God, I am so very sorry.

Then Jesus said to them, "Prophets are not without honor, except in their hometown, and among their own kin, and in their own house." (Mark 6:4)

So the other disciples told him, "We have seen the Lord." But he said to them, "Unless I see the mark of the nails in his hands, and put my finger in the mark of the nails and my hand in his side, I will not believe." (John 20:25)

23 Mark's Dream

July 2007

Mark especially likes the movies *The Wizard of Oz* and *Cinderella,* and very often he will tell me his dreams about these stories. One particular morning while he and I were in the kitchen and I was helping him shave, Mark announced: "I had a dream last night!"

I asked him, "What was it?"

He said, "Cinderella."

"Oh," I said. "Tell me what happened."

He explained the entire story with this: "She found her slipper."

I was impressed, and I wanted more. "That's great, Mark, then what happened?"

"Oh . . ." Mark said, looking down and speaking very seriously. "She melted."

But Jesus called for them and said, "Let the little children come to me, and do not stop them; for it is to such as these that the kingdom of God belongs. Truly I tell you, whoever does not receive the kingdom of God as a little child will never enter it."

(Luke 18:16-17)

24 *Instant Message*
April 11, 2007

The following is the actual transcript of an Instant Message (with only very minor edits for clarity and length) which took place late one night, during and after an especially distressing experience with a core member. I went online to find my old friend Lee Nagel, who has guided me through many harrowing experiences while in L'Arche, offering much-needed support and care. He is officially my L'Arche "accompanier"—a person chosen to offer spiritual and/or functional accompaniment on our L'Arche journey. Lee and I have been great friends since we met in 1990, when we both worked at the Catholic Diocesan offices in Green Bay. As of this writing, he is the executive director for the National Conference for Catechetical Leadership (NCCL) in Washington, DC.

Kathy: and now it might be helpful for you to pray for Joey and Mark. Joey is going ballistic as I sit here and

Mark is deathly afraid of him, and so Lisa and I both had to walk Mark up to his room, and right now Joey is in his room screaming and swearing and throwing things. It is very upsetting. Help.

Lee: I shall take a moment to ask God for quiet—I will stop and ask that Mark feel safe and that Joey quiets himself. That Mark feels safe and Joey doesn't feel threatened or threaten or lash out.

Kathy: thank you. I am still shaking. I stayed up here to see what was going on, and I heard a door open and I walked into the hallway . . . and there was Mark face to face with Joey and Mark got scared and I ushered Joey back to his room. He had been shouting and screaming and swearing and making a ruckus, and I closed his door and held his shoulders momentarily and . . . then I backed away slightly and said "Stop it!" and I closed in tighter to his face and he was turned away from me, and for the next ten minutes I talked to him, told him he sounded like a barking dog and that he was acting not at all like a man. . . . and after a few minutes I slowed my voice and calmed down and he calmed down and I just talked about being a man like the real Elvis, and not like a dog . . . and finally I had to get him to stay quiet after I left, because history shows he will start acting up again as soon as I walk away, so I said I'd make his lunch and put a cookie in there, but if I heard any noise, the cookie deal was off, and he agreed, and then he held up two fingers—two cookies, ok? I said, two cookies, ok, and I walked out . . . I came downstairs . . .

Lee: I would say that you did good—face to face, eye to eye—attention and then together we slow our adrenalin and get into sync—our heartbeat, our calmness, our oneness and then—another insight—a deal—a promise and a gift—not one earned or deserved but simply one because he is a child of God. You are good and God is with you.

Kathy: and I started to tell Lisa and she said Mark came back down and was in the living room, too scared to go back up, so I walked over and quietly said that Joey was quiet and it was safe for him to go back up, so he was okay with me not walking him back up, but he did ask, "Where are you sleeping?" and I told him, and he was OK. All is well, but I'm still shaking.

Lee: shaking is okay

Kathy: well, it was a frightful experience.

Lee: I believe that—I could hear it—I could feel it—I could sense it but I also sensed that you were not alone.

Kathy: I knew immediately when I started to calm down, that God was in the room helping me. I felt him, and your prayers too, knowing that I had just told you and you were praying. I had a strength that was not mine alone.

Lee: I love it at those moments when I can actually feel God's presence and the power of someone praying—it is such a gift and awareness that God is always there.

Kathy: I love it too. And this is what L'Arche teaches us. I just know that this message has to be told. Thanks for listening.

Lee: It is these times especially when we share God's presence in our lives that I feel most connected. I shall be praying for you and the community there, especially Mark and Joey.

Kathy: Thank you so much. Goodnight.

Lee: Peace and prayers and blessings. Goodnight.

The LORD is my shepherd, I shall not want.
  He makes me lie down in green pastures;
he leads me beside still waters;
  he restores my soul.
He leads me in right paths
  for his name's sake.
Even though I walk through the darkest valley,
  I fear no evil;
for you are with me;
  your rod and your staff—
they comfort me. (Psalm 23:1-4)

Conclusion

May 2008

Almost nine years have passed since I first stepped into Arch I with all my stuff. Many things have changed; many things have not. The most significant change in the core members is how much they have aged. On December 5, 2007, our beloved core member David Miller passed away. He was 65 and had Down syndrome. As of this writing, Gertie lives with increasing dementia and accompanying behaviors such as getting everybody up in the middle of the night to get ready for the day, walking out of the house, sitting on the lawn swing in the rain, and forgetting how to pray the nighttime litany she was known for. Marilyn and Gertie have reversed roles. Marilyn arrived at The Arch very dependent, and Gertie's maternal instincts filled both of their needs. Many people used to ask if Gertie was Marilyn's mom because of how protective she was of Marilyn. Today, it's Marilyn who helps Gertie remember her shoes and who she should be praying for at night.

We predict, sadly, that there will likely be even more deaths in the next couple of years due to the simple fact that persons with disabilities tend not to live as long as the rest of the population. Persons with Down syndrome especially live, on average, twenty years fewer than their physically healthy counterparts. We have six core members with this syndrome, three of whom are already older than the national average. The other two hover around fifty.

We are in need of more live-in assistants due to four young people who moved out of the community in 2007. L'Arche was founded on the ideal that living in peace—or at least striving for that—with persons who are very different is a small but powerful sign of hope to the world that peace is possible.

We have many assistants whom we call "live-outs" who come to "share life" with our core members during the week. These people provide very needed support for the community as they are responsible to help with the daily needs of living in a home with persons with disabilities. Live-out assistants also support the daily life of our apartment community. Six core members live in individual apartments. Some need little more than help with budgeting and shopping. Others need daily medical and other attention, but they are expected to live in a house for a year before moving into an apartment, and they join the community for monthly gatherings such as birthday parties, anniversary prayer nights, and potluck suppers.

My health has—knock on wood—been excellent. I get regular checkups and have no intention of ever getting that cancer back. As my son Aaron said to me once, "Mom, you know you have been cured from cancer when you die from something else." I'd like to die of old age, thank you.

When we gathered for a recent monthly birthday party at Arch III, where I am house coordinator, I stood before the thirty-five or so people packed into our living room, waiting for the last people to enter and find chairs, and I felt at peace. Comfortable in my L'Arche skin. How life has changed in almost nine years! I spoke with the whole group as if I were speaking to just one person in private. A feeling of belonging flooded me. This was my home and I lived with persons with disabilities and believed in the core of my being that this very act was the sign of hope Jean Vanier spoke of in 1964 when he invited Philipe and Raphael to join him in the first L'Arche community in France.

L'Arche gives me daily opportunities to see the face of God in the core members and others. I echo Jean Vanier's voice in what I have felt called to live here: "We do not have to be saviours of the world! We are simply human beings, enfolded in weakness and in hope, called together to change our world one heart at a time."[8]

L'Arche has done its job well. It has changed my heart.

The deck is still rolling. But take note. I'm still walking on it. With both feet.

Notes

[1] Henri J.M. Nouwen, *Bread for the Journey: A Daybook of Wisdom and Faith* (San Francisco: HarperSanFrancisco, 1997).

[2] Brian Kolodiejchuk, *Mother Teresa: Come Be My Light* (New York: Doubleday, 2007).

[3] Jean Vanier, *Finding Peace* (Toronto: House of Anansi Press, 2003), 8.

[4] Betty Rollin, *First, You Cry* (Philadelphia: Lippincott, 1976).

[5] Jean Vanier, *Becoming Human* (Mahwah, NJ: Paulist Press, 1998), 134.

[6] Ibid., 162.

[7] Jean Vanier, *From Brokenness to Community* (Mahwah, NJ: Paulist Press, 1992), 19.

[8] Jean Vanier, *Becoming Human*, 163.